Food Ethics

None of us can avoid being interested in food. Our very existence depends on the supply of safe, nutritious foods. It is then hardly surprising that food has become the focus of a wide range of ethical concerns: Is the food we buy safe? Is it produced by means which respect the welfare of animals and conserve the environment? Are modern biotechnologies employed in food production immoral?

This book addresses such issues by applying ethical principles to many areas of current concern. The contributors provide original and thought-provoking treatments of a number of highly topical issues – from global hunger and its ethical implications to the cultural factors affecting food consumption. This interdisciplinary study will prove to be essential reading for all those concerned with food, as professionals, students or consumers.

Ben Mepham is Director of the Centre for Applied Bioethics at Nottingham University. He has published widely in the fields of bioethics and applied biology.

Professional Ethics

General editors:

Andrew Belsey,
Centre for Applied Ethics, University of Wales, Cardiff
and Ruth Chadwick,
Centre for Professional Ethics, University of Central Lancashire

Professionalism is a subject of interest to academics, the general public and would-be professional groups. Traditional ideas of professions and professional conduct have been challenged by recent social, political and technological changes. One result has been the development for almost every profession of an ethical code of conduct which attempts to formalise its values and standards. These codes of conduct raise a number of questions about the status of a 'profession' and the consequent moral implications for behaviour.

This series seeks to examine these questions both critically and constructively. Individual volumes will consider issues relevant to particular professions, including nursing, genetic counselling, journalism, business, the food industry and law. Other volumes will address issues relevant to all professional groups such as the function and value of a code of ethics and the demands of confidentiality.

Also available in this series:

Ethical Issues in Journalism and the Media
edited by Andrew Belsey and Ruth Chadwick

Genetic Counselling: Practice and Principles
edited by Angus Clarke

Ethical Issues in Nursing
edited by Geoffrey Hunt

The Ground of Professional Ethics
Daryl Koehn

Ethical Issues in Social Work
edited by Richard Hugman and David Smith

Food Ethics

Edited by
Ben Mepham

London and New York

First published 1996
by Routledge
11 New Fetter Lane, London EC4P 4EE

Simultaneously published in the USA and Canada
by Routledge
29 West 35th Street, New York, NY 10001

Typeset in Times by Routledge
Printed and bound in Great Britain by
TJ Press (Padstow) Ltd, Padstow, Cornwall

British Library Cataloguing in Publication Data
A catalogue record for this book is available from the British
Library

Library of Congress Cataloging in Publication Data
Food ethics/edited by Ben Mepham.
p.c. – (Professional ethics)
Includes bibliographical references and index.
1. Food industry and trade–Moral and ethical aspects. 2. Food
supply. 3. Agricultural innovations. I. Mepham, T.B.
II. Series
HD9000.5.F5948 199696-2493
178–dc20CIP

ISBN 0–415–12451–4 (hbk)
ISBN 0–415–12452–2 (pbk)

Contents

Series editors' foreword

Professional Ethics is now acknowledged as a field of study in its own right. Much of its recent development has resulted from rethinking traditional medical ethics in the light of new moral problems arising out of advances in medical science and technology. Applied philosophers, ethicists and lawyers have devoted considerable energy to exploring the dilemmas emerging from modern health-care practices and their effects on the practitioner–patient relationship.

But the point can be generalised. Even in health care, ethical dilemmas are not confined to medical practitioners. And beyond health care, other groups are beginning to think critically about the kind of service they offer and about the nature of the relationship between provider and recipient. In many areas of life social, political and technological changes have challenged traditional ideas of practice.

One visible sign of these developments has been the proliferation of codes of ethics, or of professional conduct. The drafting of such a code provides an opportunity for professionals to examine the nature and goals of their work, and offers information to others about what can be expected from them. If a code has a disciplinary function, it may even offer protection to members of the public.

But is the existence of such a code itself a criterion of a profession? What exactly is a profession? Can a group acquire professional status, and if so, how? Does the label 'professional' have implications, from a moral point of view, for acceptable behaviour, and if so how far do such implications extend?

The subject matter of this volume, the production and distribution of food, is not usually regarded as a profession in the traditional sense. Yet the biological necessity of food for every individual and the cultural and symbolic roles of food in society mean that ethical issues are never far away. These include responsibilities to both individuals and society in the areas of health and safety, the treatment of animals, the provision of clear and sufficient information so that people can know what they are buying and eating, and the issue of informed consent by the public to new technologies such as genetically modified plant and animal food sources. In discussing these and other issues, this book is contributing new and important insights to public debate on a familiar subject, food, and ensuring that vital theoretical and ethical issues are not overlooked.

The Professional Ethics book series, edited from the Centre for Applied Ethics in Cardiff and the Centre for Professional Ethics in Preston, seeks to examine ethical issues in the professions and related areas both critically and constructively. Individual volumes will address issues relevant to all professional groups, such as the nature of a profession, the function and value of codes of ethics, and the demands of confidentiality. Other volumes examine issues relevant to particular professions, including those which have hitherto received little attention, such as journalism, social work and genetic counselling.

Andrew Belsey
Ruth Chadwick

Notes on contributors

Jeremy Cherfas, author of *The Hunting of the Whales* (Penguin, 1989) and *The Seed Savers' Handbook* (Worldly Goods, 1996), has a long-standing interest in the rational exploitation of renewable resources. He relaunched the Heritage Seed Library of the Henry Doubleday Research Association and has advised the European Parliament on plant genetic resources and worked with the FAO, the International Board for Plant Genetic Resources and the International Rice Research Institute.

Michael Crawford is Director of the Institute of Brain Chemistry at Queen Elizabeth Hospital for Children, London. A graduate of Edinburgh and London Universities, he researched tropical heart disease and cancer at the Medical School, Kampala, Uganda, before becoming head of the biochemistry department at the Nuffield Institute of Comparative Medicine, London. He holds a Special Professorship at Nottingham University and was awarded the International Award in Modern Nutrition in 1995.

Nigel Dower is Senior Lecturer in Philosophy at the University of Aberdeen. His research interests include the ethics of development, environment and international relations, and his publications include: *World Poverty – Challenge and Response* (Sessions, 1983). He is Director of the Centre for Philosophy, Technology and Society, University of Aberdeen, and Vice-President of the International Development Ethics Association.

Keb Ghebremeskel studied chemistry at the University of Addis Ababa and received his doctorate in nutritional biochemistry at the University of Wales. After working at the International Development Agency, he became a research associate at the Nuffield Institute of Comparative Medicine, London, and later moved to the Institute of Brain Chemistry. He has published on comparative nutrition and latterly on the nutrition of preterm babies.

Leslie Gofton is Lecturer in Behavioural Science at the University of Newcastle upon Tyne. He specialises in consumer behaviour, with special reference to food. For the past ten years, he has researched and published on changing patterns of eating and drinking, including work on marketing of alcohol and illegal drugs, food scares, and more recently genetically modified foods.

Robert Hamilton is Lecturer in Consumer Behaviour and Consumerism at the University of Lancaster Management School. He studied philosophy and theology, before moving into sociology and consumer behaviour. He has written on consumer decisions, marketing codes of practice, the perception of meals and choice of foods, and ethics in marketing.

Andrew Johnson is a partner in the White Horse Press, which publishes the journals *Environmental Values* and *Society and Animals*. He is the author of *Factory Farming* (Blackwell, 1991) and of a number of articles on animals, ethics and the environment; and editor of *Philosophy Today*, the newsletter of the Society for Applied Philosophy.

John S. Marsh CBE is a graduate of Oxford and Reading Universities. Between 1957 and 1977 he was successively Research Economist, Lecturer and Reader at Reading before moving to Aberdeen as Professor of Agricultural Economics. In 1984, he returned to a Chair at Reading. He has been Secretary, then President of the Agricultural Economics Society, has served on several public committees and chairs the Agricultural Wages Board.

Ben Mepham is Director of the Centre for Applied Bioethics and Reader in Physiology in the Department of Physiology and Environmental Science at the University of Nottingham. The Centre for Applied Bioethics is a research and teaching unit concerned with ethical issues in food and agriculture, particularly those raised by modern biotechnologies, with a focus on the exploitation of animals for food, experimentation and medical therapy.

Erik Millstone is Senior Lecturer in Science and Technology Policy at Sussex University. A physics graduate, who subsequently worked in philosophy, he was appointed to teach philosophy of science at Sussex in 1973, but has progressively moved into science policy. For the past twenty years his main focus has been on policies intended to protect public health from food-borne hazards, and more recently this has extended to consideration of broader environmental policy topics, especially those concerned with lead pollution.

Preface

Ben Mepham

It is hardly a matter of contention that there are ethical issues related
to food. We all need food, in adequate quantity and of adequate
quality, to survive and maintain health. The fact that millions of
people in the world are severely malnourished, often to the point of
starvation, while others devote substantial time and effort to losing
weight by dieting, is evidence enough that something is awry with the
ethics of food provisioning. But ethical concerns are by no means
confined to such striking examples of injustice. The production of
food in modern agricultural practice often has damaging effects on
the environment, in terms of soil erosion, chemical pollution and loss
of species. The exploitation of animals for food is thought by some to
be ethically unacceptable under any conditions and by others to
seriously infringe their welfare when animals are reared in intensive
systems. Food production, processing and marketing also have
significant effects on its safety for human consumption, and such
concerns are compounded by the adoption of modern biotechnologies which offend the public sense of propriety.

Food is so basic a human need that it readily becomes the focus or
means of expression of a whole range of other human concerns, both
beneficent and maleficent. Thus, food habits serve both to strengthen
cultural bonds and to emphasise intercultural differences: food
supply is an important element of foreign aid, but trade in food can
also be a means of subordination, or even a weapon of war. Food is
essential to the sustenance of life, but it can be a source of disease and
death.

The underlying assumption motivating the compilation of this
collection of essays is that the interrelatedness of such concerns and
their centrality to human well-being merits the promotion of an
interdisciplinary approach to food which has an explicitly normative

objective. Consideration of 'food ethics' might thus promote more appropriate ways of thinking about human well-being and autonomy, and facilitate the practical and political changes which need to be introduced if we are not only to achieve a more just global society, but indeed if we are to hand on to our successors a world which is worth inheriting.

Each of the chapter authors has addressed his subject by first identifying the social, economic or scientific issues and then proceeding to analyse their ethical dimensions. (The absence of women authors is incidental: none of those invited to contribute was able to accept.) All authors have concluded their chapters with suggestions for changes in line with the ethical principles discussed. Readers are not, however, presented with a set of 'codes of ethical practice'. Rather, they are encouraged to reflect on the ethical implications of those aspects of the food industry with which they are most directly concerned, and with their relationships to other aspects of the food chain, with a view to informing sound ethical judgements. 'Ethics' can be considered at several levels, from abstruse meta-ethical theory, at one extreme, to codes of practice, at the other. The aim here is to occupy the middle ground in which ethical theory is applied to practical concerns: but such insights need to be interpreted more explicitly in the contexts of professional practice.

Nigel Dower considers the question of global hunger from the perspective of people in Western developed countries, and in the light of FAO (Food and Agriculture Organisation) predictions that by 2010 AD chronic malnutrition will continue to afflict over 600 million people. The persistence of hunger presents a major moral challenge not only because it undermines human welfare and dignity, but because its existence is clearly avoidable. Dower examines several 'theories of obligation', each of which supports the claim that we have a moral duty to ameliorate world hunger. However, as indicated by John Marsh, the ways in which we address that task are by no means unproblematical. Food trade, being perceived as a largely self-serving activity, might seem to be ethically less worthy than provision of aid, which ostensibly expresses altruistic motives. In practice, the complications of both aid and trade undermine this simple distinction and imply that there is need for close analysis of the motives and effects of both, if we are to make progress in the alleviation of world hunger.

Ethical issues raised by food production systems are discussed by Jeremy Cherfas and Andrew Johnson. Sustainability is concerned with issues of intergenerational justice and environmental ethics, and in this context, Cherfas analyses the impacts of modern industrial agriculture on soil erosion, use of non-renewable resources and biodiversity. His proposed solutions include regionality, full-cost accounting and increasing adoption of organic systems of agriculture. Johnson surveys ethical theories relating to animals and explores their implications with respect to the wide range of agricultural uses (and abuses) to which animals are subjected. He considers more extensive and informative food labelling to be a minimum requirement for promoting 'ethical consumerism', but argues also for new legislation to outlaw unacceptable husbandry practices and to ensure appropriate minimum welfare standards.

Michael Crawford and Keb Ghebremeskel illustrate the ways in which the rapid and radical dietary changes introduced in Western developed countries have undermined consumer health, as evidenced for example by high incidences of cardiovascular disease and cancer. Unfortunately, these unhealthy diets are spreading to less developed countries, where they appear to be having similarly adverse effects. Crawford and Ghebremeskel recommend a range of strategies, from educational programmes in schools to government intervention in agricultural production, by which national diets might be improved. On a related theme, Erik Millstone addresses government policy on food safety and using the example of saccharin, compares four models of the relationship between science and ethics. He identifies the main ethical dilemma facing policy-makers as the circumstances in which the interests of consumers and producers differ, but the relevant scientific evidence is incomplete or controversial. Millstone recommends a general set of guidelines which should enable policy-makers to deal more honestly and effectively with such food safety issues.

Recently, much public concern has surrounded the employment of biotechnology in food production and processing. While some people welcome biotechnology's almost boundless potential for altering food productivity and quality, for others, those same capabilities imply an equally profound potential for misuse. As a means of facilitating ethical decision-making on food biotechnology relevant to public policy, Ben Mepham proposes a framework for ethical analysis, which is based on principles employed in medical ethics, and illustrates its use with reference to animal and plant technologies.

It is clear that both food habits and food ethics are deeply embedded in social cultures. ('Morals' and 'mores' derive from the same Latin word, meaning 'custom'.) Leslie Gofton's analysis demonstrates that food ethics needs to take account of concerns which extend far beyond the conventional 'risk–benefit' analysis. Yet we should beware of equating food ethics with a 'green politics' which simply reflects a fear of the future and disillusionment with the way Western society is developing: an authentic food ethics needs to encompass the interests of those outside Western cultural history, and that will entail a fundamental change in educational provision to promote social harmony. Cultural factors are also reflected in food marketing, and in this context, Robert Hamilton examines the ethical implications of respect for consumer sovereignty. He considers several examples of marketing practice, in the light of three principles: respect for consumer choice, capability (of exercising sound choice) and information (on which to base choice). For Hamilton, ethical quality in marketing is demonstrated by an enthusiasm for competition, an openness with information about products, and the promotion of products with 'precautionary circumspection'.

There is little doubt that many of the ethical problems related to food concern recent technological developments, and since science is perceived as a proverbial double-edged sword, it is important that research policies be subjected to ethical scrutiny. An ethical critique of current UK research policy in the agricultural and food sciences is provided by Ben Mepham, who argues that rather than pursuing the dominant reductionist programme, there is a strong case for drawing on a broader range of expertise in tackling the complex problems surrounding global security in food, health and the environment.

In many other fields of applied ethics, the types of dilemma encountered concern personal moral choices which impact quite specifically on other individuals, such as patients or clients. By contrast, almost all the issues discussed in this volume relate to universal, pervasive, long-term concerns, which are most readily perceived as subjects of public policy decisions. They are all based on the biological requirement (often unmet) for safe, acceptable, nutritious food, which is produced in ways which respect (or fail to respect) the welfare of other sentient beings, alive and unborn. Hence the issues demand attention from philosophers, economists, sociologists and anthropologists, as well as medical, agricultural and food scientists. In the author's opinion, if real progress is to be made in resolving the numerous ethical concerns related to food, these separate fields of disciplinary expertise need to be welded together in a new interdisciplinary programme, for which he has coined the term 'food ethics'. Only then will possibilities for change be understood and knowledge acquired of how to achieve it.

Chapter 1

Global hunger: moral dilemmas

Nigel Dower

MORAL CHALLENGES

At a recent conference, the prediction was made that in 2010 AD chronic malnutrition in the 93 developing countries would afflict about 637 million people. This was seen as an improvement on the figure of 781 million in 1988/9 (and 941 million in 1969/71).[1] It is, in fact, a quite shocking statistic. It represents an awful lot of people who in the next fifteen years will be malnourished or starving, many dying prematurely of these causes. We[2] have to ask ourselves the following question: if this level of malnutrition remains in fifteen years' time, will it be there because we cannot avoid it, or because we allow it to continue? To put it in a way reminiscent of Augustine's question about God and the existence of evil in the world: will it exist because we *cannot* prevent it or because we *will* not prevent it? By 'will' here I do not mean 'deliberately aim at', of course, but more modestly 'allow to happen because of policies which we know have unwanted but preventable consequences'.

I am not saying that all poverty and hunger in the future could be prevented. But insofar as the trends in the future depend upon earlier decisions – individual, institutional, political – we have to ask: could those decisions have been different so that there would have been less hunger? If they could have been, should they have been? In this chapter, I suggest that the prediction above relies on an unduly pessimistic assessment of the possibility of generous human motivation. Delegates at the United Nations Summit in Copenhagen (March 1995) on 'social development' agreed, since they adopted a ten-year plan to meet the basic needs of virtually every human being on earth.

The prediction is based on a number of assumptions – about food production, new methods of agriculture, new areas of co-operation, inputs from non-governmental organisations (NGOs) and levels of giving by private individuals. Reductions in global hunger will certainly be seen as the goal of many agents, for example, food scientists and aid officials, but also the general outcome of other developments, economic and technological.

The key question to be asked is: in addition to the efforts already being made to reduce world hunger, and assumed in the prediction, by governments, agencies, international bodies, NGOs and concerned individuals, could significantly more be done to bring about further reductions? I want to argue that much more could be done and given that it could be done, ought to be done. Governments, international organisations and businesses could do a lot more. But, beyond a small but significant degree of latitude within which officials can work, what they can do depends upon certain conditions. International organisations could make hunger/poverty reduction an even higher priority in their activities if governments agreed that they should. Governments could do a lot more if their citizens wanted them to do so. Business companies could do a lot more (for example, to make sure that their economic activities did not causes poverty or hunger) if those they are answerable to – their shareholders – determined that they should do so, and consumers of their products sent signals by their consumer preferences.

Briefly, any corporate body, whether government, business or NGO, will have certain goals and priorities and also rules as constraints on how to pursue them, and these are largely determined in the long run by their constituencies: voters, citizens, shareholders, consumers and members of pressure groups. Whether the reduction of global hunger becomes a stronger decision-making factor – either as a goal or a constraint – depends on how people, as members of these constituencies, want them to act. And this in turn depends upon how people want to live and how they think they and others ought to act.

Can people, then, act in ways that will improve on the prediction above? I suggest that they can, because the prediction is based on the premise that, whatever efforts are currently envisaged for reducing hunger, there is a continued commitment to affluence in the North, i.e. in the rich countries of the world, and thus to levels and kinds of aid programme consistent with this commitment. But if people were to accept the following three propositions, then there could be significant action (beyond that assumed in the prediction).[3] The three propositions are:

- that as moral beings we have significant duties to help other people who suffer;
- that hunger is a particularly extreme form of suffering; and
- that we should see the scope of our obligations as global.

This chapter defends these three propositions. But, it may be thought, almost everyone already accepts all three, and as a result of this a certain amount is done and supported, as indicated above. This, however, is questionable. First, to the extent that we accept them, we may still for a variety of reasons show moral weakness and do nothing or very little. Whatever theorists may say about the nature and reality of 'free will', there is an obvious sense in which people choose whether to act morally or to act otherwise, out of self-interest or immediate inclination. Second, we may not have fully grasped the implications of our moral ideas, and this is partly why an explicit enquiry such as this is of use in sharpening our understanding. Both moral motivation and moral understanding are, in any case, strengthened by reciprocity, solidarity and publicly shared values. Third, there are a significant number of thinkers who do not accept one or other of the propositions, who reject or marginalise the duty to help others, who do not see hunger as of particular moral importance, or who deny the global scope of our obligations. Whether we see such views as false or as merely unacceptable, the point remains that if such thinkers were persuaded otherwise, the potentiality for action would be much improved. The practical importance of moral education for global citizenship needs to be recognised, not just because of global poverty but because of the need for peace and sustained environmental protection.

SOME MORE SPECIFIC MORAL DILEMMAS

The key issue: limits to liberty

The most fundamental dilemma is this: how far are those of us who are not hungry, especially the rich in the Northern hemisphere, prepared to limit our rights to economic and other forms of liberty in order to facilitate the reduction of hunger?

At one extreme, there is the response of an uncompromising economic libertarian: we have no duty to help alleviate the ills of others, either general ills or hunger in particular. Beyond our duty not to harm others actively, we have liberty to pursue our own interests –

whether as individuals, organisations or nation-states. A variation of this is: the best way to reduce poverty and hunger is to stimulate general economic activity, and this happens by Adam Smith's 'hidden hand', that is, if we all pursue our own economic interests and let 'trickle down' do the rest.

At the other extreme, someone may argue that we all ought to do all we can to alleviate hunger (or more generally alleviate serious ills, of which hunger is a major part). Such an approach, which would be taking to its logical conclusion the sentiment many feel 'hunger ought not to be allowed to exist where it can be avoided', would require a radical transformation to the way we live our personal and public lives.

In the middle, there is the approach according to which we have significant duties to reduce suffering, especially hunger and extreme poverty, but not an overburdening duty to do all we can. It is this middle position which I shall be defending in this chapter.

Further issues

Should we or our governments put emphasis upon food aid, or upon the development of appropriate agricultural skills? Upon developing self-sufficiency in farmers or giving poor people other economic resources so that they can buy the food they need? Upon the introduction of new seeds or new technologies? Upon economic and social reforms within poor countries, or upon appropriate policies in international bodies? Upon strict population policies?

Many of these questions are at least partly answered by adopting certain views of the facts – about what causes what (especially in the long run), which policy is (more) effective in which kind of situation. Few would doubt that food aid in a famine is crucial, but many would argue that food aid as a way of addressing endemic undernutrition is disastrous.[4] But these questions are rarely purely factual questions. They often involve value questions as well, in that the questioner has certain priorities in mind.

One type of value issue would be: is the hunger of a famine of greater moral urgency than the hunger of endemic poverty? Put another way: is it morally more important that the international community responds to famines adequately than to endemic poverty? Perhaps the former is more manageable than the latter, but is the hunger less of an evil in endemic poverty than in famine? Hardly, I will argue, yet we often act as if it were.

A second type of issue concerns the relative importance of hunger as an ill as compared with other ills and forms of suffering. Are the other aspects of extreme poverty – diseases, helplessness, lack of dignity – on the same footing? Is poverty, even if not absolute, less of an evil than hunger? From the point of view of public policy, do hunger and extreme poverty really have priority over other goals of development, such as economic progress for all, or the maintenance and development of a healthy and vital culture, or sound legal and political infrastructure? I shall argue that hunger should be seen as having a special priority amongst the ills to be addressed by public policy, both national and international.

A third type of issue concerns the choice of policies which have as their focus the reduction of hunger but which have to be sensitive to other ethical criteria as well. Does a hunger-reduction policy enhance or undermine autonomy and self-reliance? Does an aid policy with strings attached undermine the independence of a poor country's government? Does the introduction of new techniques and seeds undermine indigenous seeds, skills and knowledge? It will be a feature of my account that we cannot see the ethical significance of hunger in isolation and that any justified policies must integrate a range of considerations together.

SOME CONTEXT-SETTING FACTUAL CLAIMS

This discussion makes the following broad set of empirical assumptions (about which I am no expert). If they are broadly right, then they provide the proper setting for the ethical arguments which follow. They are all factual claims, as opposed to value claims, but they progress from the less controversial to the more controversial.

Claim 1

A very large number of human beings are living in conditions of hunger – either outright starvation or severe malnutrition. Estimates vary, but the figure of 781 million would be seen by many as an underestimate. 'Absolute poverty', which is more extensive than hunger, afflicts about one-fifth of the world population, that is, well over one billion people.

Claim 2

It is generally understood that, whatever might be the case in the future, if populations go on rising sharply (though many predict that this will not happen), there is at present more than enough food in the world for no one to be hungry – the problem is that either the food is in the wrong places or it could easily be available given appropriate agricultural policies but is not (perhaps because other things are grown like tobacco and other cash crops). Often the food is available in the very countries where the hunger exists. Many studies attest to the claim that we have 'hunger in a world of plenty'.[5]

The reason why the hungry are hungry is that they do not have access to food, because they do not grow it, do not have the economic power to acquire it, or are not given it or the money to buy it. Without prejudging the ethical issues about possible responsibility and/or blame for this, the fact is that food is simply not distributed in the right way so that all have enough of it to avoid hunger and malnutrition.

If the hungry are to be less hungry, then one or more of three broad types of condition must apply:

(i) They grow food (and/or hunt, catch, pick it, – i.e. do something *by their own initiative* in 'mixing their labour' with hitherto unclaimed parts of the commons.[6]

(ii) They acquire greater economic power to purchase food (by barter, exchange or the money system). This means either engaging in other kinds of activity or growing other 'cash' crops for sale.

(iii) They are given food or money to buy food.

Claim 3

If the hungry are to escape from their hunger, then apart from all the efforts which the poor themselves are constantly making, there also needs to be action on the part of others – individuals, governments, international bodies and NGOs.

However, option (iii) is of limited value, except in emergency situations such as famines or natural disasters. For there are immense (non-monetary) costs involved in food aid or even the simple transfer of money for food. For instance, they create dependency, undermining development/self-reliance in the long run and distorting local markets, as well as challenging the dignity and self-respect of the hungry themselves. Hunger may be an evil, but so is the loss of dignity involved in seeking food aid. Just receiving it, even if it is not begged for, can undermine self-respect.

The kinds of activity under (i) and (ii) that are appropriate depend on local circumstances. For instance, the introduction of new seeds and techniques or new employment possibilities will be important. But so too will changes in the social, economic, political or legal framework in a country. Changes in international policies, over types of aid, debt relief or the rules of the international economy, will also be crucial.

Claim 4

Even from the above outline, we can see that the factors relevant to reducing hunger have little to do with food as such, certainly not with our transferring the food which we have to the hungry. They have more to do with economic resources, access to adequate land and possession of relevant skills.

The interconnections between affluence, poverty and hunger are complex so it is important to realise that while some of the ethical issues to do with world hunger concern eating habits in the North – what, and how much, we eat, and the methods used to sustain this – most of the ethical issues have little directly to do with this. Rather, they concern our whole way of life – how much we generally consume, what kinds of things we consume and the whole economic infrastructure underpinning our privileged ways. The question therefore is not: what is the connection between our eating well and their eating badly, but what is the connection between our living well and their eating badly? Or rather, the key question is about a broader connection, between our living well and their not living well, of which their eating badly is simply a part, if a crucial one.

We have to beware of thinking that the primary problem is that what we eat affects what they eat. This would be the collective generalisation of the thought expressed by a mother when she says to her child, 'Johnny, eat up your pudding – think of the starving in Ethiopia'. No doubt this thought has its place in moral education, but even a child will see through its logic if it is presented as a serious causal thesis. Its role is more symbolic, a way of reminding us how fortunate we are and how we should somehow be in solidarity with the rest of humankind.

WHAT FEATURES OF HUNGER MAKE IT MORALLY SIGNIFICANT?

Before we look directly at the question of why we ought to do something about hunger, we need to consider a prior question: what is it about hunger which makes it a bad state of affairs to be in?

The evils of hunger

We can identify the following factors, all of which are bad. Hunger involves physical pain and suffering, loss of vitality and energy, lack of health in the body, in particular current illnesses and diseases, and a proneness to these conditions. It leads to maldevelopment, physically and mentally, especially in children, early death, directly or via diseases and illness or greater proneness to accidents, loss (or lack) of control over one's life to a high degree, plus associated feelings of helplessness. Because of its primacy in terms of the need to avoid hunger, it involves an extreme form of poverty through lack of resources for pursuing meaningful activities in life. It involves loss/lack of dignity/self-respect.

The evils of extreme poverty

Even without hunger, extreme poverty can be a very bad state to be in for a number of reasons. It involves disease, illness and disability. There are two features of this: on the one hand, a greater proneness to these conditions anyway (because of poor housing, less varied diet and low spending on preventative medicine), and on the other hand, fewer resources to tackle these conditions when they occur. It involves physical suffering of various forms (apart from hunger), and a lack of control over one's own life or a sense of being a victim rather than an agent. This may stem from a general feeling of powerlessness or from the fact (and perception of the fact) that one is oppressed/exploited/discriminated against by those with greater power (economic, political, legal). It involves psychological suffering from one's own perception of one's standing in society – either from a sense of rejection by others or from a sense of injustice over the gross inequality of wealth around one. It involves a lack of quality of life, stemming from the sheer struggle to survive plus the lack of resources to spend on 'quality of life' activities. It involves the likelihood of an early death (through illness, stress or accident).

Clearly, the ills of hunger are not generally different from the ills of poverty (even without hunger), but they usually occur in a more acute form. Hunger in this sense is the index of extreme poverty. But the various features of hunger which make it an evil requiring an ethical response are also the general characteristics of extreme poverty (even without hunger).

On this basis, there might not seem to be anything special about hunger from an ethical point of view. Yet, this seems wrong, since the obligation to alleviate hunger seems to be in a category of greater ethical urgency. Why might one think this?

Reasons for the special status of alleviating hunger

Two kinds of reason may be given for saying that hunger has a special moral status. Neither, on its own, shows hunger to be uniquely different from other kinds of evil, but the combination gives it a special status so far as the normal setting of priorities for action ought to be concerned.

First, if people are hungry, they are in a condition which undermines the possibility, or at least the likelihood, of their achieving other aspects of human well-being; that is, not being hungry is one of the preconditions (normally) of achieving other aspects of human well-being – enjoyable activities, control, relatively little suffering and the exercise of choices.

Second, there is an important sense in which the evil of hunger is more readily avoidable than most other evils. If a person is hungry because he or she does not have access to food, it only takes others to provide it. Except for famine situations, 'lifeboat scarcity' situations or other forms of isolation, it takes only the intervention of others who are aware of the situation to enable a person to have food. Within a community where there is enough food for all, and an awareness of who is or may be going hungry, the evil of hunger can be alleviated by the actions of others; indeed in most societies in the past, which by modern standards were not materially affluent, that at least would have been done, however much uncontrollable diseases may have afflicted and killed many.

The irony is that in the modern world, with our extensive knowledge of global hunger, our extensive communication and transportation systems and the existence of food surpluses, we do not seem to be able to replicate the practices of past smaller societies of at least trying to ensure that everyone has enough of the one crucial thing it is in the power of others to provide – namely food. It is as though we have the technical ability to do so, but lack the psychological and institutional capacities. This is, of course, an over-simplification, but it suggests that there are two related factors which are missing. We do not see ourselves morally as a global community or society in which those who are well-off have at least a minimum commitment to ensure, as far as is possible, that all have access to this precondition of human well-being – adequate food. Second, the reason why we are psychologically and institutionally unable to meet the challenge is because most of us are not sufficiently persuaded by a moral vision that tells us that this is really a pressing thing to do. What we need is a global ethic which spells out the idea that we have serious obligations towards all other human beings, obligations which cross societal and national frontiers.[7]

THEORIES OF OBLIGATION

A Kantian approach

Onora O'Neill has presented a modern Kantian approach which can be summed up as follows: hunger and extreme poverty undermine the proper development and exercise of rational agency.[8] They do so because the very poor are often subject to coercion and deception (which fails to respect their rational agency) and more generally because extreme poverty deprives the poor of real autonomy. This requires us as moral beings to respect the poor as fellow rational agents in two ways: first, we must not deceive or coerce them, or be beneficiaries of others (such as multi-national companies) who deceive or coerce them, and we must take action to prevent such coercion and deception (via, for example, political action). Second, we must act so as to enable the poor to develop and exercise their rational autonomy by appropriate action (political as well as individual acts of helping) – this is what is required by material justice.

The difficulty with this appealing position is that it locates the evil of hunger in the lack or loss of rational agency. Now this is clearly an important part of what hunger does to the poor (a part often neglected), but it is equally distorting to omit mention of the sheer physical suffering, disease, physical malfunctioning and disability, which are themselves also inherently evil.

Benevolence

Peter Singer famously suggested the following principle: 'If it is in our power to prevent something bad from happening without thereby sacrificing anything of comparable moral importance, we ought, morally, to do it'.[9] The principle has been the subject of much discussion.

How should we read this? Insofar as he was thinking of death (by disease/starvation) – parallel to the child drowning in the pond whom a passer-by is able to rescue – the assumption is that death is an evil and that, if it is wrong to cause death (by killing), by the same reasoning it is wrong to let death occur when it is preventable. Whatever it is that makes death a bad thing to happen (at least before old age), makes the principle operative.

But Singer's point is a broader one than that. As a Utilitarian he sees the prevention of evil much more generally, as including both the prevention of suffering and the prevention of the continuation of suffering when it is already there. On this basis, hunger (as well as disease and poverty more generally) causes much suffering as well as causing death. Given Singer's principle, then, one ought to prevent hunger so long as one is not sacrificing something of comparable moral significance. Arguably, the contribution of one's money to the pleasures of one's own well-being or that of one's friends or family does not outweigh the amount of evil reduced, so generally one ought to seek to prevent hunger, if one is at all affluent.

Again there are several problems with this approach taken on its own. First, it characterises the evils of poverty and hunger in terms of suffering. Arguably, this is only part of the picture; other things are important, not only the emphasis upon the undermining of rational agency (stressed by Kantians) but also the fact that disease and hunger are bad in themselves, not merely insofar as they give rise to suffering. (If one stressed the duty merely to prevent death, that would be an even narrower basis for saying hunger was bad, since it is an evil because of the state of the hungry whilst alive – having to submit to suffering, weakness and indignity.)

This approach also locates the focus of the moral duty in the wrong way. Suffering is reduced merely because it happens to be part of the overall good which one can do in the world (and would be overlooked if it was not). But, arguably, people in need ought to be helped because *they* are in need, not because on balance more good is done in the world by helping than by not helping.

The strength of this position, however, is that it is built on a universal and appealing feature of human psychology – benevolence (sympathy, charity, love and caring). Almost all moral theories have some place for the duty to care for others in general beyond the spheres of special relations (family, friends and contracted services), that is, for the idea of 'negative responsibility' or responsibility not to let bad things happen which one could prevent.

But the feature of Singer's position which has caused much discussion is the 'as much as you can' feature – the ethics of radical sacrifice. Neither the Kantian theory nor any of the other three I will consider (functioning, human rights, contract) makes this claim explicit, but they can be read in different ways – as requiring extensive action or merely a significant amount of caring. So the issue is worth considering now. Ought we to do all we can to alleviate suffering? Many would answer 'no'. Two kinds of factors are often noted: first, one has special relations (to one's children, one's spouse, one's friends, one's community) which take priority over any duty of general caring (even if more 'good' could be done in the world if one did the latter). Second, we have rights (some might say duties to ourselves) to pursue our own interests, to have our own projects, even to do things for pleasure out of inclination. There is, as one writer puts it, 'a robust zone of indifference'[10] where what we do is neither morally required nor morally forbidden.

On the other hand, there is a significant duty of caring and contributing to the well-being of others. But there is no precise formula for determining how much, in what ways and to whom. Many factors will enter into determining what an individual decides he or she ought to do – temperament, circumstances, knowledge, reciprocity and support from others, not least a recognition that such caring is consistent with and conducive to one's own well-being. (If someone had an overwhelming passion for expensive sports cars that took up all his cash and time such that he 'could not' choose to act for the sake of others, we would be inclined to say, I think, that there was an imbalance in his life that undermined his real well-being as well as obscuring a real dimension to his being as a moral agent.[11])

Functioning approach (Aristotelian)

A latter-day Aristotelian position is developed by Sen, Nussbaum and Crocker.[12] A full human life consists of the development of a range of capabilities and their exercise in appropriate functionings. Functionings include not merely being adequately fed and healthy, but also the exercise of rationality, practical skills, sociability, liberty, etc. If one has any concern at all for the well-being of others, then one will be concerned about the removal of hunger, both because bodily functioning through proper and adequate nutrition is in itself important, and because hunger undermines the proper functioning or exercise of most other human capabilities.

The virtue of this approach is that it gives us a full account of what human well-being is, and corrects the one-sidedness of both Kantian and Utilitarian theories. Its Aristotelian vision of political order or society is committed to ensuring that all its members are able to exercise their capabilities and thus have access to what is necessary for this. (This does not, it should be noted, entail egalitarianism or even a uniform account of what material resources are minimally required, since that could vary with situation and individual.) It also provides us with one way of understanding why we should care for the well-being of others: if we belong to the same society or political community as others, then we will have reason to care for them.

The challenge for this theory is this: why should I care for the well-being of distant peoples who do not belong to my society or political community? The answer here is to develop an account of human beings as living in one global society or community. We need therefore a version of cosmopolitanism (a theory of world citizenship).[13] Let us consider two further theories and see if they help us with the cosmopolitan dimension.

Human rights theories

If a human right is a right held in virtue of our nature by all human beings unconditionally (not dependent on the laws or customs or decisions of human beings), then if there are human rights, we clearly have a framework for general obligation to promote or protect them. Much depends on what we identify as human rights and how we understand the framework of correlative duties that surrounds them. Henry Shue has usefully suggested that there are three socially basic rights – to subsistence, security and liberty.[14] These are basic because they are essentially preconditions for the exercise of other more complex rights. There are, according to Shue, three types of duties corresponding to such rights – duties not to deprive, duties to protect from standard threats of deprivation, and duties to come to the aid of the deprived.

Such an approach, in stressing universal rights, certainly makes little sense unless we suppose a global framework of obligation. As Shue says, 'socially basic rights are the minimum demand of all humanity on all humanity'.[15] He does not, however, advocate a radical redistribution of wealth from North to South. We are back to the issue of 'how much'. In a society of abundant resources and with no or few outside obligations (as countries in the North tend to perceive themselves to be), everyone can reasonably fulfil their duty to aid the deprived, but on a global scale of 781 million hungry, the picture is very different. But there is no doubt that human rights discourse puts pressure on governments and individuals to accept duties both to protect from deprivation and to aid the deprived on a global scale.

Contractarianism

Rawls' *A Theory of Justice* provides a powerful account of social justice within an organised society under one political authority.[16] If a society is seen as a scheme of co-operation amongst individuals who all agree to the distribution of benefits and burdens, Rawls argues that a set of principles which would be fair to all and agreed by all in an ideal contract would include commitments to equal liberty and to what he calls the 'difference principle'. The latter claims that only those differences in wealth would be justified which enabled the least well-off to be better off than under any other arrangements. Although Rawls allows for significant differences in wealth (to allow for incentives for productive activities of benefit to everyone), the tenor of his theory is egalitarian.[17]

Rawls' theory has been adapted by other writers, such as Beitz[18] and Pogge,[19] to fit the global scene. If the whole world is seen as one society, then the same principles ought to apply to the world as a whole: we would have a global 'difference principle', and thus an argument in the name of social justice for massive redistribution of resources. Beitz recognises that this belongs to 'ideal theory', and that we are far from being able to realise it, because of the lack of a sense of global community and the lack of appropriate international institutions. Nevertheless, it provides a goal towards which we should move and a vision of one global moral community.

Rawls' theory is immensely attractive, particularly insofar as the general conception of social justice says that it is reasonable for any person, as a member of society, to expect society, as a matter of justice, to protect their socially basic rights (in Shue's sense). The extension of it to the global scale is both natural and important, suggesting that social justice applies to the world as a whole as a 'welfare world', in which for instance aid might be seen as a global income tax. Such contract theories are also useful in showing that we are more likely to help others if we see ourselves as part of a reciprocating scheme of social co-operation. On the other hand, it does not seem right to say that our obligations to other human beings depend on such arrangements – on implicit contracts, on assurance of reciprocity or there already being a world community.[20] Our obligations to other human beings (and indeed other forms of life) more simply rest on our capacity to affect their well-being – for good or ill.

ARE WE DOING ENOUGH?

I have surveyed a number of different theories, each of which in their own way supports the claim that we have duties to help alleviate world hunger (but only in appropriate ways, since food aid is only a limited part of the appropriate repertoire of responses).

Are we in the North doing enough? Clearly not, if we mean 'enough to get rid of world hunger'. Are we doing all we can, even if that is not enough? Clearly not. As individuals most people in the North could do much more in one way or another. Although governments operate within constraints of public opinion, clearly, within the leeway which they have, they do much less than they could.

If, as I have argued, it is not the case that we ought to do all that we can do, are we doing all that we should? Arguably, far from it! There are several arguments for this. First, many people simply do not accept the appropriate ethical framework (one of the above theories, for instance) because they are libertarians, or they deny the global scope of (serious) obligation. Second, many other people may accept the framework in which duties to alleviate hunger are acknowledged (including a duty to support and promote one's government's doing the same), but they do not act on it (very much) because of one or both of two factors: the sense that efforts to alleviate hunger are largely wasted and the feeling that those around them do not affirm what they are doing or act in solidarity. Third, many people have an unduly restrictive conception of their own overall well-being, which they see as incompatible with helping others.

If we are to do all we should, then I believe that there is much work to be done on all the fronts indicated. That is, vigorous argument is needed against libertarian thinking and anti-global thinking, extensive work is needed in establishing effective aid programmes and making more publicly known the successes that are already achieved, in creating appropriate social climates of mutual support for such work, and in spreading the recognition that the expression of global citizenship is not contrary to one's real interests.[21]

NOTES

1 From ESS (FAO, 1992) and 'Agriculture towards 2010' (FAO, 1993), quoted in Daws, M., 'The food gap – trends in the developing world', *Nutrition, Food and Farming in the Developing World*, (Aberdeen, Boyd Orr Research Centre, 1994).
2 When I use the term 'we' I have in mind primarily citizens in the Northern hemisphere, but the issues are of relevance to people in countries in the South too, especially those who are well-off (which includes most of those who would be reading a chapter like this!).
3 It should be noted that all three claims need to be accepted as true, since denial of any one and acceptance of the other two could lead to inaction so far as global hunger is concerned.
4 Garrett Hardin was famous (or notorious) for questioning the long-term utility of food aid. See e.g. Hardin, G., 'Lifeboat ethics – the case against helping the poor', in Aiken, W. and La Follette, H. (eds) *World Hunger and Moral Obligation* (Englewood Cliffs, Prentice Hall, 1977). Most of the articles make the case for aid. It is still a useful collection on the issue (though a new edition with new contributions is forthcoming).
5 This is the subtitle of the May 1995 number of *The New Internationalist*. Consider also the very useful book, Robinson, C., *Hungry Farmers* (London, Christian Aid, 1989).
6 Stealing is logically another option but, for obvious reasons, is both a marginal as well as a morally problematical solution.
7 Apart from increasing interest theoretically in a 'global ethic', much emphasis is now put on 'global citizenship' in education. See, however, the controversy caused by Martha Nussbaum's leading article 'Patriotism and cosmopolitanism', *Boston Review*, XIV (5), October 1994.
8 O'Neill, O., *The Faces of Hunger* (London, Allen and Unwin, 1986).
9 Singer, P., 'Famine, affluence and morality', *Philosophy and Public Affairs* (1971 – reprinted in several books). See also a more extended version, 'Rich and poor' in *Practical Ethics* (London, Cambridge University Press, 1979).
10 See Fishkin, R., 'Theories of justice and international relations: the limits of liberal theory' in Ellis, A. (ed.) *Ethics and International Relations* (Manchester, Manchester University Press, 1986).
11 I am indebted to Ben Mepham for this example.
12 The best source for this is David Crocker's extensive exegetical articles on Sen and Nussbaum's work in 'development ethics', especially Crocker, D., 'Hunger, capability, and development', forthcoming in Aiken, W. and

La Follette, H. (eds) *World Hunger and Moral Obligation*, 2nd edn (Englewood Cliffs, Prentice Hall, 1995).

13   Nussbaum herself has been keen to develop the theory in this way. See e.g. her lead article in the *Boston Review*, October 1994. Kant's theory and Utilitarianism are also of course forms of cosmopolitanism.

14   Shue, H., *Basic Rights: subsistence, affluence and US foreign policy* (Princeton, Princeton University Press, 1980).

15   Ibid., p.19.

16   Rawls, J., *A Theory of Justice* (Oxford, Oxford University Press, 1971).

17   He does not however talk in terms of hunger or extreme poverty, because the assumption is that the minimum position in society would be significantly better than that.

18   Beitz, C., *Political Theory and International Relations* (Princeton, Princeton University Press, 1979) Part III.

19   Pogge, Th., *Realising Rawls* (Cornell University Press, 1989) Part III.

20   If 'world community' means no more than 'all human beings who are bound by moral duties to one another', then, yes, we are part of a world community, even if most people do not recognise it.

21   A somewhat different treatment of these issues can be found in my chapter 'World poverty' in Singer, P. (ed.) *Companion to Ethics* (Oxford, Blackwell, 1991) and a longer treatment in Dower, N., *World Poverty Challenge and Response* (York, Sessions, 1983).

Chapter 2

Food aid and trade

John S. Marsh

Food aid and trade are both means by which food produced in one country may be consumed in another. In terms of the volumes and products affected trade is very much larger than aid.[1] In some desperate situations aid provides the only means by which people facing starvation as a result of natural or man-made catastrophes can survive. The driving forces of trade and aid are radically different. Trade reflects the attempts of participants to maximise the value they derive from the assets they control. Aid is driven by a mixture of humanitarian and political motives; it involves governments, international institutions as well as many voluntary agencies.

Trade, being largely a self-serving activity, might appear less worthy, in moral terms, than aid, which embodies altruistic motives. In practice, the complications of both trade and aid make it less clear that aid is superior. This chapter sets out some of these complications, dealing mainly with trade and then, very briefly, with aid. In doing so it raises, but does not resolve, many ethical questions. Those concerned to do right cannot escape from the need to analyse motives and effects when they engage in either trade or aid.

TRADE AS A 'VIRTUOUS ACTIVITY'

The conclusion of the most recent round of negotiations in GATT (the General Agreement on Tariffs and Trade) was hailed as a major step towards improving the operation of the world's economy. Various estimates were made of the potential increase in global wealth which would occur because of the reduction in barriers to trade.[2] A substantial part of the total gains arose from changes in agricultural trade.

The logic which lies behind this enthusiasm for trade is deeply rooted in the assumptions of classical economics. Within that framework of ideas, value is determined by individual preferences revealed by the ways individuals spend their money. Improvements in the functioning of the economic system mean that individuals are able to choose a bundle of goods and services which they value more highly than others. Markets play a central role because they enable people to exchange goods or services for others. Modern industrial societies depend upon a high degree of specialisation. By permitting people to concentrate on a limited range of activities, in which they have or acquire special skills, markets ensure that their ability to consume far exceeds that which would be possible if they had to produce every item they required themselves. Extending markets will bring increased benefits by creating greater opportunities for specialising in those tasks for which the individual or country is best fitted. These benefits do not require any improvement in technology or increased natural resources; they arise from the process of trade itself. Because people are made richer, it is also likely that the stock of man-made resources, that is capital, will be increased. In the long term, this is a potent means of raising real income levels.

There are no reasons within this logic for placing any barriers in the path of trade. Obstacles to trade must be regarded as morally as well as practically objectionable. Those who oppose greater freedom, as do agricultural lobbies in many developed countries, are regarded as acting in a self-interested manner, to the detriment of society as a whole.[3] International trade is no exception. Indeed since, within the food sector, the relative availability of natural resources varies more within the world than within any one economy, there is every reason to ensure that no avoidable obstacles are placed in the path of freer trade.

Following this logic, recent progress in liberalising world agricultural trade is a moral as well as material improvement.

WHAT GOES WRONG?

Despite the considerable efforts to liberalise trade between countries, there remain many doubts as to whether more trade is either materially or morally virtuous. Economists, politicians and many private citizens have questioned the claims made for freer trade. Their reasons vary but many apply with especial force to agriculture and the food sector. Some of these doubts are now discussed.

Employment and the pains of structural adjustment

The simplest versions of trade theory assume full employment. When competition from imports forces a business to close, its resources move to the next most rewarding use. The extra output in the new use is added to the real income of the economy as a whole. Thus the full benefits of trade are realised only when such structural adjustment is complete.

In the real world, adjustments are neither instant, nor painless or cost free. Trade in agriculture and food implies substantial structural change. In the late nineteenth century there was a sharp decline in farming in the UK. Elsewhere in Europe, Denmark and the Netherlands adapted their farming, concentrating on high-quality fresh livestock and horticultural products. Over much of the continent however, governments were less ready to accept structural change. They introduced policies which encouraged domestic self-sufficiency and protected the 'family farm'.[4] Underlying these responses was the belief that, if competition were allowed from countries where land and labour was cheaper or the climate more favourable, only a small number of farmers would remain in business in Europe. Change on this scale would cause unacceptable hardship for farmers and their families, rural society would be destroyed and established political balances upset.

This argument can be questioned. In the European Union less than 6% of the workforce is in farming. Structural change has taken place. Farmers in Europe have a greater ability to compete. Resistance to change imposes high costs on consumers and taxpayers. Despite this, the wish to preserve the family farm still dominates political attitudes. It reflects other values than those assumed in the free trade model.

Externalities, environmental issues and 'public goods'

Trade in foodstuffs often involves costs which do not figure in the accounts of those directly involved. For example, increased exports may necessitate the use of more pesticides. However, these may contaminate water systems. As a result, water users face additional costs to acquire water that is fit to drink. Conventional trade accounts take note of the increased returns from agricultural exports, but they do not take account of the resource cost of cleaning polluted water supplies.

Such costs or benefits are called 'externalities' by economists. In an ideal world policy would ensure that both producers and consumers faced the full cost of the decisions they take. In the real world such fine tuning is beyond the capacity of policy-makers. Not only are there technical problems of evaluation, but appropriate policies are likely to face strong political opposition. The neglect of such issues means, however, that it is impossible to come to reliable conclusions about the overall gain or loss to the economy from trade.

Agricultural expansion as a result of trade may give rise to a variety of such externalities. The UNCED[5] conference, held at Rio in 1992, drew attention to possible environmental consequences.[6] There are many potential risks: for example, deforestation, loss of wildlife, reduced biodiversity, pollution and soil erosion. Less tangible but equally real, agricultural change may damage treasured landscapes and diminish the recreational value of the countryside. Trade, by changing the location of production, may add to or diminish such losses.

Uncertainty and risk

Major fluctuations in supply or price impose real hardships, especially on the poorest consumers and the least viable farmers. Trade may affect this either because of its effect on the volume of food available or through the operation of currency markets. Trade may either lessen or intensify uncertainty in supply. The more widely food production is dispersed the less likely are supplies to be vulnerable to crop failures caused by drought, pests or diseases in any one region. In contrast, if trade concentrates production on a limited number of low-cost areas, crop failures may lead to dramatic price increases. Trade exposes supplies to the risk of political or military intervention. Many have argued that food security demands domestic production.[7] Others have made much of the unreliability of imports.[8]

The fact that trade between countries involves exchanging currencies exposes producers and consumers to uncertainties arising from fluctuations in international money markets. Such changes can dramatically affect the viability of farm businesses.

Trade may expose consumers to risks arising from products made to different standards. Increasingly food is sold in processed form. Consumers may not know from what raw materials it is made or whether it is safe. Governments have sought to help consumers through regulation, labelling requirements, setting and monitoring standards and making food sellers responsible for the safety of their

wares. However, standards differ among countries so the risks
consumers face may increase when products cross frontiers. Through
the Food and Agriculture Organisation of the United Nations (FAO),
the international community has developed the Codex Alimentarius
to provide reassurance that food crossing frontiers is safe.[9]

Imperfections in competition

The balance of power between participants in a market is of moral as
well as practical importance. Traditional trade theory, grounded in
notions of perfect competition, assumed that no individual buyer or
seller could affect market prices by altering the amount they bought
or sold. In this sense, both sides were equally impotent. Viewed from
the point of view of an individual farmer or food consumer this may
not seem unrealistic. However, there are some participants in the
market whose decisions do affect its working, notably governments
and large, multi-national enterprises. Government policies are considered separately later in this chapter. Here some of the issues which
arise in relation to the private sector are briefly discussed.

Commodity food trade, particularly trade in cereals and oilseeds, is
dominated by a small number of international traders. In the area of
processed foods, a few multi-national food companies account for a
very large proportion of the market. Such large organisations exercise
considerable influence within the market. They may do so through
acquiring better information and analysis than smaller companies
can afford. They often make major investments, sometimes in low-
income countries, to build vertically integrated businesses linking
production with the final point of sale. In small economies their
investment and wage policies can play a major part in determining the
people's standard of living.

Trade, which enables such companies to function on a global scale,
also justifies the considerable effort which many of them make in
research and development. This both opens up new opportunities for
using resources productively and tends to consolidate their position
within the market. This power can be considerable. Governments in
modern democratic societies are usually held to have a duty to look
after the interests of the weak. Multi-national companies can, to a
degree, escape their power, because business may be relocated to
places where governments are more compliant. In principle, international agreements and regulations should provide a more satisfactory
balance between local interests and multi-lateral corporations. In

practice, as will be discussed later, such agreements are fragile and often ineffective.

Economists have long recognised that if markets are not competitive the optimum use of resources is unlikely to result. A powerful argument for liberalising trade is that consumers benefit because local businesses face more competition. To ensure that competition within the EEC[10] was not frustrated by anti-competitive behaviour the Treaty of Rome devoted a chapter, articles 85 to 94, to setting out rules governing competition.

Economic and ethical issues are closely intertwined in such a situation as this. Large-scale enterprises achieve economies of scale not open to smaller firms. Multi-national companies bring skills and capital needed to make resources in host countries productive and improve the incomes of their people. Thus, even though the executives of such firms have to operate to maximise the benefit to their own companies, the countries in which they work also benefit. Governments and critics have to judge whether the disadvantages of this relationship outweigh the gains. There can be no general answers.

Governments, agriculture and trade policies

Governments have many reasons for intervening in agricultural trade. Secure food supplies are seen as a primary responsibility. International markets are regarded as dangerously volatile. Imported food is alleged to impose strains on the balance of payments. Even where trade is not the object of agricultural policy, it is likely to be affected. Attempts to moderate structural change, to take account of externalities or to shield vulnerable groups of consumers or producers are likely to affect the level of trade.

In most rich countries, agricultural policies have protected farmers. Internal prices have been kept high either by subsidies or by controlling the amount available on the domestic market. Where more has been produced than can be sold at home, export subsidies have been made available. Measurement of the extent of such support is complex but the most useful guide is given by OECD's (Organisation for Economic Cooperation and Development) measures of PSEs (Producer Subsidy Equivalents) and CSE (Consumer Subsidy Equivalents).[11]

These policies, especially when major countries engage in competitive dumping, depress world market prices and lead to a wasteful use of global resources.[12] Low-cost agricultural exporters lose traditional markets not only in the countries concerned but wherever dumped exports reach the world market. It also means that countries seeking to develop their agricultural sectors are denied access to markets in which they could compete.

It is difficult to justify such support on moral grounds. It makes taxpayers or consumers, or both, in the country concerned poorer. Support for domestic production forces structural adjustment on farmers in other countries. Most of the benefit of high prices goes to large farmers and landowners. Entry to the industry is made more difficult for poor, young people. High, stable support prices encourage technologies which may damage the environment. Far from helping rural communities to survive, which depends on establishing new income-earning activities, protection traps resources in noncompetitive farm businesses.

For food-importing developing countries, intervention in agriculture focuses more on the need to hold food prices down than to support farm incomes. From their point of view, the excesses of developed country agricultural policy may be a positive advantage. Matthews argues that trade liberalisation, much favoured by orthodox economists, would work to the disadvantage of the developing world.[13] To hold food prices down governments have over-valued exchange rates and placed taxes on food exports.

In the short term, such policies benefit the urban population at the expense of agriculture and the rural community. In the long term, they may disadvantage both. Agriculture remains the major economic sector in most developing countries, contributing to economic growth both by increasing its own productivity and by releasing labour to newer industries. If investment is discouraged productivity may lag and all sections of society suffer. Where such policies increase dependence upon imports, they may expose the country concerned to uncertain world prices and greater balance of payments difficulties.

Famine and food trade

For many people, the sight of starving children is convincing evidence of the failure of the world's food system to meet acceptable ethical standards. Trade may make some situations worse but it may also play a major role in removing the threat of hunger.

Famine occurs not just because supplies are scarce but because those affected have too few entitlements to bid for the food which is available.[14] It is an outcome of poverty or war rather than of crop failure. When food is scarce, trade may intensify difficulties. Faced by food shortage, richer people are able to pay more. Thus, in the depths of famine, food may be exported by poorer regions where shortages may be life-threatening. During the Irish Potato Famine, food continued to be exported despite the desperate hunger of a poor local population.[15]

Although trade may exacerbate problems when famine occurs, it may also be an essential component of any long-term solution. Trade can enable populations to improve their incomes based on their skills and non-agricultural resources. Growth stems from access to export markets for the whole range of potentially tradable products, not just food. Since the ability to survive depends more on income than on food production, trade plays a positive role.

Trade and conspicuous waste

Food products of broadly similar character are often simultaneously exported and imported by the same country. Fresh food is flown from other continents to tickle the fancy of consumers. Common-sense critics claim that this is not needed and results in a conspicuous waste of resources. Things may not be so simple. First, subtle differences in the qualities of food products may make their value to consumers exceed the cost of transport. Second, food may utilise air transport which would otherwise be empty. In this case the trade makes productive a resource which would otherwise have been idle.

Such common-sense objections implicitly challenge the morality of consumer sovereignty. They are based on values other than willingness to pay. Other systems also have their pitfalls. The decline of communism in the former Soviet Union and Eastern Europe, and the adoption of market mechanisms in China, suggest that values determined by governments or bureaucrats may be even less acceptable. Governments should seek to ensure that consumers face the full costs of the decisions they make rather than override consumer choice. Intervention beyond that may be justified only for a limited set of outcomes which are agreed to be morally unacceptable, such as the trade in drugs.

Food trade and equity

Equity plays a major role in much ethical debate. Market economies lead to inequitable outcomes. The ability to consume depends more on accidents of birth, location and time than on the efforts or merits of individuals. International trade displays these inequalities on a global scale and trade in foodstuffs is not exempt from this tendency. As a result of trade, consumers in poor countries may see local resources used to pander to the tastes of overfed foreign consumers; and small producers may find their incomes depressed by competition from larger businesses elsewhere in the world.

Modern food production relies increasingly on capital and scientific skills rather than manual labour. Employment tends to fall[16] despite increasing output. Farm workers are replaced by capital equipment and purchased inputs. As a result, trade can widen the gulf between rich and poor people in the same economy and between rich and poor countries.

Ethical anxieties about such outcomes do not lead to straightforward solutions. Government intervention in the allocation of resources has often been a failure.[17] Attempts to 'preserve the family farm' make food production more expensive and involve barriers to trade which damage domestic consumers and overseas suppliers. Those who suffer most from such interventions are themselves relatively poor.

To offset the effect of such protectionist policies, some countries offer special terms to developing country exporters. The EU, for example, offers preferential terms under the Lomé Convention. Many critics claim that such countries would gain even more from a reduction of agricultural protection in Europe.

If people are unable to buy food they cannot survive. If they cannot afford a satisfactory diet they are likely to be ill. Thus, even though there may be a general willingness to allow market forces to allocate incomes and determine production, special arrangements are often used to ensure that poor people have access to food. These include rationing systems, the provision of free or subsidised meals and activities such as the US Food Stamp programme. The parallel in the international context is the provision of food aid.

Food trade, consumer and producer responsibilities

Ethics demands consideration of responsibility for the consequences of action. Trade ensures that, in aggregate, the decisions of consumers determine how resources are used in their own and other countries. Consumers may take account of the impact of their spending on producers and on the environment. However, although such individual discipline may be of moral worth, effective action depends upon changing overall behaviour. Voluntary organisations often seek to persuade people to act in a responsible manner, for example in recycling waste and supporting low-income producers.[18]

Exhortation may have limited results. Those concerned about undesirable impacts of trade frequently seek legislation to constrain consumer behaviour. Development charities campaign for governments to provide more aid and increased preferential access for developing countries' food exports. Environmental lobbies seek rules requiring suppliers to recover used cans or bottles. Ethical concerns about the impact of trade in live animals have been at the forefront of agricultural policy debates in the EU.[19]

Food trade as a 'weapon'

Sieges have a long history. Depriving an enemy of food is a means of bringing him to heel. Trade sanctions attempt to attain similar goals. The effectiveness of food as a weapon has been contested.[20] However, to avoid vulnerability many countries attempt to ensure a higher level of self-sufficiency in essential foodstuffs than is consistent with free trade.

Preventing imports from a foreign supplier may also be used as a weapon. Campaigners opposed to apartheid sought to discourage the import of fresh fruit and vegetables from South Africa. Exporting countries usually find means of evading such restrictions but they are likely to involve added costs and lower prices.

The use of food as a weapon raises questions about the morality of penalising consumers or producers for government actions over which they have no control.

International agreements and food trade

Trade in food is affected by a many different types of international agreement. There are world-wide agreements such as GATT or

CITES (the Convention on Trade in Endangered Species), regional agreements such as the EU and NAFTA,[21] special arrangements relating to developing countries, bilateral arrangements between countries and international commodity agreements relating to specific products. Such arrangements might be visualised as devices to rectify the failings of free trade.

In this context their performance is not reassuring. National interests differ, and agreements risk being undermined by 'free riders'.[22] In an article on Agriculture and the Uruguay Round,[23] Guyomard et al. stress that agricultural trade policies are basically a function of domestic policy considerations. This will be readily understood by those engaged in trade negotiations. The implicit ethical position is that it is right for a government to pursue the interests of its own citizens regardless of their impact on other countries.

This must disappoint those who see international agreements, such as GATT and its successor, the WTO,[24] as a nascent form of international government, dealing with matters of general concern to humanity. Such organisations are better understood as arenas within which deals are made by the most powerful players. Weaker countries exercise influence by forming alliances and cultivating the support of the major powers.

There have been many proposals to reform international trade in order to diminish the disadvantages of poorer countries.[25] In practice little progress has been made. The world's major trading nations have not accepted such proposals. This is not necessarily because individual negotiators are unaware of, or indifferent to, the plight of many poor countries: it is primarily because they are required to give priority to the interests of those whom they represent.

International commodity agreements have been designed not to free but to regulate markets.[26] Their record has been disappointing. Two major problems make it difficult to operate such agreements. First, there is the likelihood that there will be trends in market prices because of changes in the conditions of demand or supply. These result in persistent tendencies for market prices to bump against the floor or the ceiling of any agreed range. In falling markets, importing countries pay more for products within the agreement than outside. When prices are strong, exporters would receive more from non-adherents to the agreement. Thus national interests encourage breaking or leaving such agreements. A second difficulty arises if the policy succeeds in raising long-term prices above trend clearing prices. This is likely to encourage the use of substitutes and new entrants not constrained by the agreement.

FOOD AID

Within a world dominated by national interests, aid provides a means to offset some of the disadvantages of poorer countries. Food has often been used as aid. Outrage at the sight of starving children and the existence of food stocks for which no commercial market exists have made this acceptable to the public opinion in donor countries. There are, however, other motives, for example, a wish to exercise political influence or to build up new export markets. These relate to very different moral perceptions.

For many people, food aid is wholly altruistic. They support aid agencies because they wish to help people who are facing hunger or starvation. NGOs (non-governmental organisations) play a vital role. They create awareness in rich societies of the need for aid. They do not just send food but promote improved food production and distribution within recipient countries. They act quickly in famine situations, where official agencies may face more bureaucratic procedures. They promote development of the economy as a whole. They often work within countries with powerless people who may be missed by official aid. Both national governments and international agencies work with NGOs, which are often efficient distributors of aid, and which can avoid political difficulties which may impede direct government involvement.[27]

Whilst food aid provided by governments may be an expression of the altruism of their electorates, other motives often influence its direction.[28] This plurality of motive makes it impossible to come to any general conclusion about its morality. Evidence suggests that the volume of food aid depends more on the extent of surpluses than on the need of recipients. For example, the FAO Annual Review for 1993 reported that following a reduction in stock levels, cereals aid had declined by 23% compared with the 1992/93 harvest year.

Even though aid may be conditional upon supporting donors' national interests, arguments used to justify it vary. Economists Mellor and Johnston[29] point to the role of agriculture in development, arguing that donor countries will benefit from larger export markets which result. Others argue that the purpose of aid should be to support donors' existing policies, such as the disposal of agricultural surpluses. Aid may be used to help firms, based within the donor country, to compete with third country suppliers and the locally based producers. Governments often link aid to political support by the recipient or to the provision of military facilities.

Such justifications are far removed from ethical positions based on 'rights theories'. These would claim that rich countries should not supply their own citizens with higher food rights whilst the subsistence rights of poorer countries are not met. They are also distant from a Rawlsian approach,[30] which would allocate aid on the basis of the needs of the least fortunate. Individuals, pressure groups and government ministers all use rhetoric which stresses that food aid is offered in response to need. Aid provision is much more readily understood in terms of the national interests of donors.

In economic terms food aid is a relatively inefficient means of providing food. Where aid originates from the excesses of agricultural protection in rich countries, the food costs more, in resource terms, than an equivalent quantity bought from the most efficient producer in a competitive market. It is likely to use more resources than would local production. Food is perishable and bulky. Considerable costs are involved in transport and distribution. These are likely to be highest in poor countries, where the infrastructure of roads and communications is poor and where there may be serious risks of food being wasted or stolen before it reaches its intended consumers. The food provided is usually produced in the donor countries – wheat and milk powder, for example. This may require changes in local diets and lead to wastage.

Such problems suggest that aid would be better provided in the form of money than of food. Increasing food security, in the long term, depends upon economic development. Improvements in the productivity of local farming may play a key role. There is a risk that food aid will be counterproductive. Neither governments nor the private sector may have much incentive to invest in local agriculture if external supplies are provided free. Aid may also create a growing dependence upon imported foodstuffs, exposing the economies of the countries concerned to volatile international markets.

Aware of the potential conflict between food aid and development, but equally alert to the fact that it may be politically easier to provide aid as food than as money, governments and aid agencies have sought to use food to support development. Used to reward labour and mobilise resources which would otherwise have been idle, such aid can result in the provision of facilities which support the growth of other economic activities. Maxwell *et al.* in a study of the effect of food-for-work in Ethiopia show how careful project design can avoid many of the disincentive effects of food aid.[31]

TRADE AND AID: OPPORTUNITIES FOR IMPROVEMENT

The conclusion of the GATT Round and the results of the UNCED conference of 1992 represent modest steps towards making world agricultural trade more liberal and more sensitive to environmental impacts. Their most important effect may be to have put these issues on the agenda of future international negotiations at which more progress may be made.

The benefits of reducing barriers to trade are long term. Whilst they are unevenly distributed among individuals and between countries, they do create a real increase in global wealth which, if the political will exists, should enable all to gain. If hardship for declining sectors is to be avoided, freer trade and greater respect for the environment need to be accompanied by support for structural adjustment within countries. Not only would this diminish individual hardship but it would hasten the time when the gains from these policies were realised.

The same logic applies to the provision of aid to development between countries. It is, however, much more difficult to justify in terms of national interest. There is a major job for voluntary agencies to inform and persuade people that aid from rich to poor countries is in the interests of the donors as well as of the recipients. There is also a crucial need for international agencies to identify and articulate the global interest and demonstrate how resources entrusted to them promote it. This implies that to allow trade to bring about its rewards we need aid. Aid is needed to remove anxieties among many less developed countries about freeing markets and to reward them for responsible attitudes to the environment. Part of the aid may continue to be in the form of food. Increasingly, however, the sort of aid offered should be determined by its efficiency in attaining the desired result, not simply by the unintended surplus production of rich countries. As the GATT settlement and the UNCED commitments may make all parties more aware of the real cost of food, they may provide, too, a foundation for a more rational approach to the use of food as aid.

NOTES

1　The largest component of food aid is delivered in the form of cereals. However, in the mid-1980s aid accounted for only 5% of total cereal imports. For the lowest income developing countries it accounted for more than half imported cereal supplies. World Bank, *World Development Report, 1988*, New York, Oxford University Press, 1988.

2　GATT estimates of the total benefits from the liberalisation of trade range from $109 to $510 billion. The World Bank estimates a gain of $213 billion: see *Impact of the Uruguay Round on Agriculture* (FAO, 1995).

3　See, for example, Williams, G.W. and Parr Rosson III, C. (1992) 'North American Free Trade Agreement provisions for agriculture', *Choices* 7, n.4. They argue that labour-intensive sectors of US agriculture may be at risk whilst cattle, hogs, grain and oilseeds should do well. Much of the debate about the merits of extending trade is conducted in terms of such effects on specific industrial sectors rather than on the economy as a whole.

4　See Tracy, M., *Agriculture in Western Europe: challenge and response, 1880–1980*, 2nd edn (London, Granada, 1982), for an excellent account of the response of European governments to the challenge of food imports.

5　United Nations Conference on Environment and Development (UNCED), 1992.

6　United Nations Organisation, *Earth Summit '92: The United Nations Conference on Environment and development, Rio de Janeiro 1992*, Quarrie, J. (ed.) (London, Regency Press, 1992).

7　The treaty establishing the European Economic Community (The Rome Treaty), Article 39 1(d) states that one of the objectives of the Common Agricultural Policy is 'to guarantee regular supplies'.

8　The short-lived ban on soya exports imposed by the US in July 1973 was sometimes held to justify considerable support for oilseed production within the EU.

9　The Codex Alimentarius Commission, instituted by the FAO in collaboration with the World Health Organisation (WHO), has the task of defining international food standards. Its proceedings constitute the Codex. Codex Alimentarius Commission, *Codex Alimentarius/joint FAO/WHO food standards programme: FAO/WHO, 1992–1994*.

10　EEC – the European Economic Community, 1958. Since 1968, following the Merger Treaties, the EEC is usually referred to as the EC, European Communities. After the Maastricht Treaty of 1992 the terminology changed to EU, European Union.

11　For an account of these measurements, see *Agricultural Policies, Markets and Trade Monitoring and Outlook* (OECD,1992). PSEs measure the value of the monetary transfers to farmers from consumers of agricultural products and from taxpayers resulting from agricultural policy. CSEs represent the implicit tax paid by consumers as a result of market price support, net of any subsidies to consumption extended as part of agricultural policy. In 1991, net percentage PSEs varied from 4, for New Zealand to 80, for Switzerland. Among major players, the EU's PSE was

49, Japan's 66 and the United States' 30. The highest percentage CSE was
−72, for Finland and the lowest −3, for New Zealand. Figures for the EU
were −42, for Japan −46 and for the US −19.

12 In the 1980s, international trade in agricultural goods became a battle-
ground between the protectionist policies of the European Community
and the United States of America. To protect its market share from
subsidised European exports, the US introduced its own Export En-
hancement Program.

13 Matthews, A., *The Common Agricultural Policy and Less Developed
Countries* (Dublin, Gill and Macmillan Ltd in association with Trocaire,
1985).

14 For an account of thinking on hunger and its causes see Drèze, J. and Sen,
A., *The Political Economy of Hunger* (Oxford, Clarendon Press, 1990);
and Griffin, K., *World Hunger and the World Economy* (London,
Macmillan, 1987).

15 Sen, A., 'Food, economics and entitlements', in Drèze, J. and Sen, A.,
op. cit.

16 In the European Union, for example, 13.5% of total civilian employment
was in agriculture in 1970, but by 1992 this had fallen to 5.8%.

17 In Italy, for example, early post-war land reform policies led to the
expropriation of 800,000 ha of land belonging to big estates and the
creation of small family holdings of 3 ha to 20 ha. Within a relatively
short period policy changed direction and attempted to enlarge small
owner-operated farms. Nearly 1,350,000 ha was involved in such policies
between 1948 and 1963 (*OECD Agricultural Policies, Markets and Trade:
monitoring and outlook, 1992*, Paris, OECD, 1992).

18 For example, the Fairtrade Foundation based in London claims to offer
a 'people friendly' label that guarantees a better deal for Third World
producers.

19 An important recent case before a GATT panel was the tuna/dolphin
dispute between the United States and Mexico. The United States
introduced legislation to ban the import of tuna from Mexico because
the fishing methods used by Mexican exporters led to the destruction of
large numbers of dolphins. The Mexican government successfully challenged this restriction as a discriminatory impediment to trade. The
panel did uphold the right of the US government to require all tuna to be
labelled according to the method of production involved.

20 See for example, Thompson, P., *The Ethics of Aid and Trade* (London,
Cambridge University Press, 1992), chapter 1, where it is argued that
food is not effective as either a tactical or a strategic weapon.

21 NAFTA – North Atlantic Free Trade Area.

22 For example, a 'free rider' would be a country which offered marginally
more favourable terms than the international regulations allowed to
attract a larger share of investment or trade.

23 Guyomard, H., Mahe, L., Munk, K. and Roe, T.L., 'Agriculture in the
Uruguay Round: ambitions and realities', *Journal of Agricultural Economics* 44, 1993.

24 WTO – World Trade Organisation.

25 See for example Cathie, J., *The Political Economy of Food Aid* (Aldershot, Gower, 1982); and McCord, W., *Paths to Progress* (New York, W.W. Norton and Company, 1986). In 1949 an International Commodity Clearing House was proposed to promote the balanced expansion of world trade in agricultural products. This was rejected by the FAO Conference. Proposals by the Freedom from Hunger Campaign (1961) that an international agency should be set up to hold buffer stocks were also rejected. In 1974 the UN General Assembly called for a 'New Economic Order'. In the 1980s the Brandt Commission called for improved aid to poor countries but there has been little response.

26 Among the major commodities for which such agreements have been negotiated are wheat, sugar, coffee and wool.

27 For example, the International Fund for Agricultural Development, IFAD, lists 12 NGOs with which it co-financed a total of 16 projects between 1978 and 1992. The sums involved represent a very small proportion, about 1%, of the organisations' total spend but they may have permitted assistance to be given in places where more official interventions would have been resisted (IFAD Annual Report 1992, Rome).

28 See Griffin, K., *World Hunger and the World Economy* (London, Macmillan, 1987), chapter 9.

29 Mellor, J.W., *The New Economics of Growth: a strategy for India and the developing world* (Ithaca, Cornell University Press, 1976); Gale Johnson, D., *Population Growth and Economic Development: issues and evidence*, D. Gale Johnson and R.D. Lee (eds) (Wisconsin, University of Wisconsin Press, 1987).

30 See Rawls, J., *Political Liberalism* (New York, Columbia University Press, 1993).

31 Maxwell, S., Belshaw, D. and Lienso, A., 'The disincentive effect of food for work on labour supply and agricultural intensification and diversification in Ethiopia', *Journal of Agricultural Economics*, 45, 1994. Also on this theme see Clay, E.J. and Singer, H.W., 'Food aid and development issues and evidence', WFP Occasional Paper 1985; and Fitzpatrick, J. and Storey, A., 'Food aid and agricultural disincentives', *Food Policy* 14(3), 1989.

Chapter 3

Sustainable food systems[1]

Jeremy Cherfas

INTRODUCTION

Just what constitutes sustainable agriculture? There are probably as many definitions as people thinking about the subject; most agree that sustainable practices do not deny future generations their livelihood. One of the prime distinctions between various approaches to the question of sustainability seems to be the number of 'future generations' people are willing to consider. Five generations, 100 years, or 50? Or 5000? Agriculture itself is probably only 10,000 years old at the most, a span of some 5000 generations. Is it reasonable, or even possible, to think that far ahead?

The National Farmers Union in the UK states that 'there is no agreed definition' but goes on to say that 'the debate is essentially about how today's use of natural resources will affect their availability and use tomorrow, and the action necessary to protect natural resources for future generations'.[2] It is therefore somewhat astonishing to discover that the government of the United States' definition of sustainable agriculture indicates that it should 'make the most efficient use of non-renewable resources'.[3] What level of use of a non-renewable resource can ever be considered sustainable?

Even in the absence of an agreed definition, people have tried to come up with measures of sustainability. Scientists at the Institute of Arable Crops Research recently published the outcome of a close look at the long-term records of the Rothamsted Experimental Station.[4] They suggest that economic sustainability requires two criteria to be met: the trend of an economic index reflecting the ratio of output revenue to input costs must be non-negative over time; and output revenues must exceed input costs. For plots that go back to the mid-nineteenth century input:output ratios and an economic index could be calculated. These showed clearly that the plots were indeed economically sustainable.

But, as the Rothamsted scientists admit, economic sustainability as conventionally assessed gives no insight into the sustainability of the system as a whole. This requires assigning costs to aspects of the environment that are not normally valued in monetary terms, such as clean water and soil. In a first attempt to cost these externalities, the group assigned environmental costs proportional to the cost and quantity of the inputs, and included these in recalculations of the input:output ratios and economic index. The study indicated severe shortcomings with this approach: assigning proportional costs does not describe environmental effects that accumulate over time or that appear only after some threshold has been reached. There are other methods for assessing sustainability in the wider sense, for example using an array of system health indicators, but these have not yet been explored fully.

A conclusion of this study is worth quoting in full:

> while the methods for assessing economic sustainability (ignoring externalities) of an agricultural system appear to be well-understood and to behave in a reliable manner, there is no adequate method of including externalities into the assessment. If agricultural sustainability is indeed a desirable goal, further work is required to investigate appropriate methods of evaluating externalities so that the sustainability of any system can be assessed properly.

While waiting for such methods to arrive, and without arguing over a definition of sustainability, we can attempt a less quantitative approach to the fundamentals and simply ask whether current agricultural practices can indeed be sustained into the future.

Rather than struggle to achieve (or, indeed define) sustainability, I believe it is more practical to reduce unsustainability. If we seriously consider the long-term consequences of existing agricultural systems we have to conclude that they are not, in fact, sustainable. In the rest of this chapter I will argue that point for some of the most important inputs of agriculture.

SOIL

It has been estimated[5] that since 1700 some 1.2×10^9 ha (1.2 thousand million hectares) has been brought into cultivation as cropland world-wide. Much of this has been at the expense of forested lands, which have decreased by 0.9×10^9 ha in the same time. Grasslands and pasture have, by contrast, remained more or less constant since 1700, but with large regional differences: in Europe, North America and South East Asia grassland and pasture has been converted to cropland, but this has been matched by increases in pasture elsewhere, such as in Latin America.

Since 1950, statistics gathered by the Food and Agriculture Organisation of the United Nations indicate continuing expansion of croplands except in Europe, where there has been a 5% decline caused mostly by urban expansion and the abandonment of un-productive areas.

The loss of the soils that support agriculture has several causes, many of them directly related to agricultural practices. Deforestation, overgrazing, poor management of irrigation and inappropriate farm-ing techniques all take their toll of soils, as does industry. GLASOD (the Global Assessment of Soil Degradation) has estimated the extent of soil degradation under four headings: light, moderate, strong and extreme. 'Extremely' degraded soils are no longer suitable for agriculture and are beyond restoration; 'strongly' degraded soils no longer permit agriculture, needing a change in management systems to do so again and major engineering works to restore the terrain; 'moderately' degraded soils support only greatly reduced productivity and require major changes in land management systems to restore their functioning; 'lightly' degraded soils allow agriculture with a small decline in productivity and can be restored with a change in land use practices.

Since 1945, according to GLASOD, 10.5% of the Earth's vegetated area has suffered extreme, strong or moderate degradation. That amounts to 1.2×10^9 ha, coincidentally equivalent to the total area brought into cultivation since 1700. An additional 749×10^6 ha is 'lightly' degraded and could be restored. In percentage terms, Europe is the most badly affected by soil degradation, with 16% (158×10^6 ha) in the three worst categories, and only in Europe is industrial activity a significant cause of soil degradation. In absolute terms, Africa and Asia are the most degraded, with 321×10^6 ha (14.3%) in Africa and 453×10^6 ha (12.1%) in Asia. Africa suffers most from nutrient loss, poor management of irrigation, and overstocking of livestock, while Asia's problems are water and wind erosion.

In the UK, soil erosion is not thought of as a problem. The National Farmers Union paper on Sustainable Agriculture[6] says baldly, 'there are no general soil erosion problems in the UK,' while conceding that there are local problems and unsuitable use of soils in some areas. A classic textbook[7] of agriculture in the UK contains not a single reference to soil erosion as such. And yet estimates of soil loss in my own county of Somerset alone put the rate at about 4 tons per acre per year.

In the United States, soil erosion today is worse than during the Dust Bowl era.[8] In 1934, it was estimated that the United States was losing about 3×10^9 tons of soil a year. In 1972, the figure was 4×10^9 tons a year, and there was less land in production in 1972 than in 1934. The economic costs of soil erosion in the US alone have been estimated at $44 billion a year in 1992 dollars.[9] The same study indicates that erosion increases the cost of production by about 25%. World-wide, the cost of erosion is said to be $400 billion a year, about $70 per person.

These figures on soil degradation and loss ought to speak for themselves. If soil, the very foundation of agriculture, is being depleted at a rate that exceeds its rate of formation, the practices that result in that depletion are unsustainable. It is enlightening, therefore, to look at mainstream views of soil loss.

In the US, the Soil Conservation Service (SCS) was established in the wake of the dust clouds of the 1930s, its brief to minimise soil loss through erosion. Until 1979, the SCS estimate of the average rate of loss of soil was nine tons per acre per year.[10] In 1980, this figure was revised downwards to five tons per acre per year, but the SCS figure remains one of the lowest available: other estimates of average loss range between eight and twelve tons.

These figures mean little in the abstract. An inch of soil covering an acre weighs about 150 tons. At nine tons a year, it takes sixteen years to lose an inch of soil. How long does it take to make an inch of soil? Under natural conditions, estimates vary from 300 to 1000 years. In agricultural systems where organic matter is allowed to accumulate and fertilisers (dependent in most cases on fossil fuels) replace nutrients removed in harvested biomass, an inch of topsoil still takes 30 years to create. The SCS reckons that an 'acceptable' rate of loss on deep soils is five tons per acre. Over 80% of typical farms in the US Corn Belt were losing more than five tons per acre in 1974, and a detailed study of farms in Iowa reported that farms on ordinary land were losing between 40 and 50 tons/acre a year, while those on unprotected slopes were losing 200 tons/acre a year.

On a timescale of years, the loss of five tons/acre a year – an inch every 30 years – may seem acceptable. Policies have been put in place to minimise soil erosion, but often to limits that make sense only over a relatively short future. As long as there is a net loss of soil, no matter how small and no matter how deep the soil is to begin with, it is going to run out.

NITROGEN

Soil erosion removes more than the substrate that anchors plants. It also removes nutrients, and the cost of replacing them is one of the greatest costs of erosion, about $3 per ton of soil lost.[11] Of the three main nutrients – nitrogen, phosphorus and potassium – I will concentrate in this section on nitrogen, not only because it is generally the limiting nutrient, but also because its manufacture is about ten times more energy intensive than phosphate and potash.

Efficiency of ammonia manufacture (from methane and air) has fallen markedly over the past half century, from more than 350 MJ per kg of ammonia in 1930 to less than 25 MJ per kg in 1980. Partly as a result, the use of nitrogen fertilisers has increased sharply, especially in the developing world. Despite the decreased energetic cost of fertiliser manufacture, increased utilisation means that fertilisers have become the predominant input into agriculture and account for almost half the total energy used in world agriculture.[12]

Biologically, nitrate is made available to plants almost exclusively through the fixation of atmospheric nitrogen by land plants; this accounts for some 100 Tg nitrogen per year,[13] while fixation in marine environments adds another 5–20 Tg nitrogen and atmospheric lightning probably less than 10 Tg. Total 'natural' nitrogen fixation is thus about 115–135 Tg each year. Industrial nitrogen fixation for agricultural uses amounts to more than 80 Tg per year, internal combustion engines add 25 Tg a year, and legume crops (for example, clover, alfalfa, field beans and leguminous trees such as acacia) contribute about 30 Tg a year. Thus at least as much nitrogen is now fixed by human activity as by background natural processes, and in the UK the use of fertiliser nitrogen is about five times greater than biological fixation. The spread of nitrogen fertilisers is a very recent phenomenon; Vitousek estimates that half of all the industrial nitrogen fertiliser used up to 1992 was used after 1982.[14]

Quite apart from the energetic costs of manufacture, the massive use of industrial fertilisers raises other questions of sustainability. What happens to all that nitrogen? It has the potential to alter the chemistry of the atmosphere, affecting levels of greenhouse gases and of ozone. Excess nitrate leaches into water systems, reducing water quality, and must be removed. Ecologically, nitrogen is often a limiting nutrient; the addition of nitrogen reduces biodiversity and can enhance ecosystem instability, and in some places (such as the Netherlands) the unwitting fall-out of nitrogen from intensive farming is often on a par with the amount used deliberately – up to 85 kg per ha per year.

Plants that are good at using excess nitrogen are often thought of as 'weeds' that require yet more inputs to counter. Valuable species, such as edible fungi, may be driven out of non-cultivated ecosystems. The yield of less diverse ecosystems often fluctuates more wildly than that of diverse ecosystems: another unpredictable outcome of excess nitrogen. Predators and parasites can be affected too. The tissue of over-fertilised plants is often soft and sappy, making the plants more attractive to pests.

I can only hint at the unsustainable ramifications of excess nitrogen use, with no space to go into detail or into the social impacts of an agriculture that depends on bought-in fertilisers. Evans[15] and Vitousek[16] both provide ways into the labyrinth; my main point is to indicate that current use of nitrogen fertilisers is almost certainly unsustainable.

GENES

The sustainability of current policies on genetic resources is much harder to quantify and possibly more assured. That is to say, modern agriculture does not threaten genetic resources to the same extent that it threatens soil, water and energy resources. Genetic resources, as they impinge on agriculture, are all but impossible to measure anyhow. Advances in the direct manipulation of DNA bring all species within the purview of breeders of plants and of animals. As a result, every species that becomes extinct might take a potentially useful genetic sequence with it.

Concerns about sustainability and genetic resources fall into several classes. One is the disappearance of valuable genetic traits, caused by the advance of agriculture itself. This scenario looks back at plant breeding's dependence on farmers' landraces[17] and the wild and weedy relatives of crop plants as a source of agronomically important characteristics. It observes, too, that the genetically uniform modern varieties that emerge from breeding programmes carrying those characteristics are often promoted as part of a reforming package of more intensive agriculture. As a result, the very farmers' varieties that contain the valuable traits are no longer grown and so are not available to sustain future breeding programmes. It is compared, in one study, to digging up the foundations to build higher walls.[18]

The reality is somewhat different. Subsistence and traditional farmers do not always abandon their own varieties completely.[19] They may deliberately allow crossing between old and new varieties, just as they encourage crossing between wild relatives and crops. And, despite the many legitimate concerns that have been expressed about the whole enterprise of so-called *ex-situ* conservation (a term I personally feel has no relevance in the case of cultivated crops), many samples of genetic resources have been collected and stored in gene banks.[20]

Although the agricultural world needs to pay more attention to the erosion of genetic resources by the dissemination of modern uniform varieties, the process is perhaps not as immediate a threat to sustainability as it has been portrayed.

Another class of worries is that of the increasing dependence on fewer crops that are themselves genetically more uniform. The key issue here is food security, which is threatened by epidemics of pests and diseases and by instability of yield.

Simple biological principles indicate that genetically uniform populations are more at risk of attack. No matter what the basis of their protection, large populations of rapidly reproducing pests and diseases are bound, sooner rather than later, to evolve neutralising mechanisms that overcome any defence. When they do so, if the entire crop shares the same genetic material, the entire crop is vulnerable. Epidemics, rather than outbreaks, become the rule.

The first such epidemic we know of dates back 150 years, to the arrival of late blight (*Phytophthora infestans*) in Europe in May 1845. All the potatoes of Europe succumbed because all were descended from two original introductions that had no resistance to blight. One consequence was the Irish Potato Famine, in which at least a million died and a million more emigrated. The famine was the first epidemic enabled by genetic uniformity, but similar, entirely preventable, epidemics can occur in most crops all the time. They are kept at bay only by the lavish use of pesticides; potatoes receive more fungicide than any other food crop.

This points to another concern, that the use of modern, genetically uniform crops requires farmers to use other, non-sustainable inputs.

Critics point out that the so-called high-yielding varieties (HYVs) of the Green Revolution are not, in fact, high yielding. They are high response. That is, given cultivation on good land with fossil-fuel powered machinery, large amounts of nutrients, sufficient irrigation, and chemical protection from the epidemics that threaten them, HYVs respond by giving a higher yield than traditional varieties. But traditional varieties perform better without the additional inputs. The use of traditional varieties is thus more likely to be sustainable, especially if the varieties can be enhanced through breeding pro-grammes with goals that are themselves sustainable.

Genetic diversity, in and of itself, promotes healthy crops, not only for subsistence farmers but also in intensive, mechanised agriculture. There is another great advantage to the use of genetic diversity within crops and on the whole farm: it stabilises yield and often enhances it.[21] Several mechanisms are at work here. Polyculture of different species within the same field makes more efficient use of resources such as light, groundwater and nutrients. Genetically diverse mixtures of single crops prevent the epidemic spread of diseases and reduce the selection pressure on pathogens. It is impossible to predict which strains of a pathogen will dominate in any one season; a diversity of hosts will suffer a little loss each season, but overall yield will be more assured than if the farmer tries to guess which will be the best single variety to plant. For all these reasons, and others, genetic diversity is more sustainable, not least because it minimises risk of failure rather than maximising production.

WORTHLESS RULES

Those, then, are a few of the ways in which agriculture is currently unsustainable. There are many others that I have not considered (water, effluent, fuel, transport, etc.) and each of them influences all the others. Is any code of conduct or set of rules likely to make a difference to this state of affairs?

Codes of conduct are a substitute for trust. If two people know one another as individuals and are likely to continue to interact in future they should be able to carry on their relationship on the basis of mutual trust and without reference to a book of rules (other than those rules accepted by both as constituting good behaviour). It is when they do not know one another that rules, suitably policed and enforced, can be valuable and allow people to put their trust in a sticker or symbol rather than in another person.

Rules can also act as an antidote to thought. In the treatment of aphid infestations, for example, organic guidelines offer 'qualified acceptance' of the use of pyrethrum,[22] because it is made by a flower. The guidelines forbid the use of pirimicarb, because it is made by a chemical engineer. But pyrethrum, although 'natural' and 'organic,' is a broad-spectrum pesticide that kills not only aphids but also the ladybirds and hoverflies that prey on them, to say nothing of many other creatures, good, bad and indifferent. Pirimicarb, although 'unnatural' and 'synthetic,' is much better targeted, killing only aphids and leaving other creatures untouched. If one must treat an infestation, which substance better complies with the fundamental tenets that organic farmers would probably say they espouse?

It is, I hope, clear that I personally have no great faith in rules systems to permit or encourage sustainable agriculture. The conflict between pyrethrum and pirimicarb (which is but one of several similar inconsistencies in existing organic guidelines) could be quite easily resolved, but others are far more intractable and offer scant hope.

In 1993, an outbreak of *Fusarium* head blight on wheat and barley cost growers in the US an estimated \$1bn in lower yields and poorer grain quality.[23] Several factors conspired to cause the epidemic: prolonged summer rain and fungal matter on the crop residues left on the surface to protect soils from erosion permitted the fungus to attack genetically uniform plants that were not allowed the luxury of crop rotation.

Fusarium also causes stalk rot in corn. Decades ago farmers in Iowa and the Corn Belt abandoned wheat and barley as unsustainable in rotation with corn precisely because *Fusarium* spores on corn stalks made head blight a near certainty in following crops of wheat and barley. Now the sustainability of wheat and barley in other parts of the US Midwest is threatened by a set of rules designed to assist sustainability. Conservation tillage, which is compulsory if farmers want to receive government grants and subsidies, provides the perfect winter refuge for *Fusarium*.

Rules are not going to turn a fundamentally unsound prairie agriculture into a sustainable food-producing system.

SOLUTIONS

It would not be right to castigate current agriculture without offering at least some suggestions of how it may be made more sustainable. Some obvious steps to reduce the unsustainability of current practices are the introduction of a carbon tax on fossil fuels and reducing market incentives to over-exploitation (e.g. headage payments and production subsidies). But apart from these there are two other strategies that would automatically improve the long-term prospects for agriculture, namely, regionality and full-cost accounting. Unfortunately, both are rather easier to theorise about than to put into practice.

At its best, an agricultural system derives all its inputs from its immediate locality and the locality is supplied with all its needs by agriculture within its territory. A small-scale mixed farm, for example, can recycle animal waste to fertilise crop fields and use some of the crops for the animals, as food and as bedding. An exclusively arable unit needs to import its nutrients and export its waste, as does an exclusively livestock unit.

Taking this slightly further afield, geographical regions could be more self-sufficient than they have become. Campaigners have drawn attention to the phenomenon of food miles, of the distance travelled by, in one case, parsnips grown in Western Australia to fill a two-month gap in the parsnip supplies of a supermarket in Britain. Do consumers really consider themselves deprived if they cannot buy parsnips 52 weeks a year?

Specialisation, which goes hand in hand with decreased regionality, is often justified on grounds of efficiency. It costs less to grow grain in the east of England and grass (turned into meat and milk) in the west, even though the two types of commodity cross one another's paths to reach their final markets. But the main reason that this is perceived as efficient is because existing tools for measuring efficiency say it is. Hand in hand with regionality must come full-cost accounting. This too remains a vague concept, and despite the hints at an approach in my earlier reference to work at Rothamsted, nobody yet has any good idea of how full-cost accounting could be made to work or what it would comprise. It includes, however, the idea that the price of a bag of fertiliser ought to include an element that pays for removing excess nitrates from water; that shifting produce around the globe is far too cheap because the entire population pays the price of congestion, of poor air quality, of global warming, of the transport infrastructure; that farming for the best subsidies is no way to decide land use priorities; and that soil washed from the land must eventually be dredged from rivers and harbours.

As with regionality, arguments for full-cost accounting sound polemical and unsubstantiated. That does not mean that they do not hold at their core the essence of a more sustainable agriculture. I have tried to show a few of the ways in which some aspects of agriculture are, today, highly unsustainable. But there is more at issue than individual practices; the attitudes that underlie so much of modern agriculture themselves foster unsustainability. A comparison brings this out.

The International Rice Research Institute (IRRI) in the Philippines has done more than almost any other organisation to ensure that people today have enough to eat. Thanks to its efforts, the amount of rice available has continued to increase despite there being more mouths to feed and less land on which to grow food. It is no exaggeration to say that millions of people owe their lives to IRRI and the improved varieties it created, varieties that enabled the Green Revolution, which started with wheat, to take root in the rice-eating world. But, recognising that advances must be swift just to stay in the same place, IRRI recently committed itself to the development of a new super-rice.

The new variety was conceived to carry the Green Revolution forward, specifically designed to improve performance in areas where even the best modern varieties fall down. It has robust and heavy stems, capable of supporting larger ears that carry more grains of rice. Stems are fewer, but more of them bear ears. The leaves are thicker, greener, and fleshier, to feed the increased amount of grain. The root system is smaller, capable of supplying the plant but not competing with the grains for resources. And in the first harvest of grain from one prototype of this new kind of rice, yields were indeed increased by 25%. Widely planted, the super-rice could increase yields by 100 million tons per year. Extrapolating from existing individual consumption of 200 kg a year, IRRI's chief breeder says that the new varieties 'would feed at least 450 million more people'.[24]

And then what? IRRI's approach is typical: attack the component parts, increase their efficiency, reap the reward. Buy enough time to do it all again.

Outside Salinas, Kansas, in the heart of the American prairies, another research institute is also trying to change agriculture. But, rather than seeking to create more of the same, The Land Institute's goal is a completely new kind of agriculture. The idea is to work with nature, rather than against it, but to persuade nature to provide more of what people need, and to do so by creating a new type of growing system modelled on the prairies.[25]

To paraphrase Wes Jackson, founder of The Land Institute, the prairie is a polyculture, modern agriculture a monoculture. The prairie conserves soil and sponsors its own fertility. Modern agriculture squanders soil and imports fertility. The prairie runs on sunlight, modern agriculture on fossil fuel. Research has thus been directed at creating a perennial prairie polyculture. Several candidate species have been selected from four broad classes of plant: cool-season grasses, warm-season grasses, legumes, and sunflowers. These have been grown in combinations of increasing complexity and shown to over-yield. That is, combinations of two or more candidates are more productive than each grown on its own. Pressure from pests and diseases has been shown to be lower in the polycultures. Stability and resistance to invasion are currently being assessed in long-term trials. Enormous amounts remain to be done, but at present the signs are hopeful.

Offshoots of The Land Institute are examining other aspects of increased sustainability. A nearby community is measuring energy flows through it and trying to promote ideas of regionality and full-cost accounting, while an experimental farm is attempting full-cost accounting of all its inputs and outputs to determine whether it is possible to run a productive agricultural enterprise on sunshine.

That is the essential element that sets The Land Institute's approach apart. Rather than ask how we can tinker with the existing system to make it produce more (making it less unsustainable is seldom a goal), it asks whether it is possible to devise a system that is sustainable: one that runs on sunshine.

CONCLUSION

The difficulty for me, as a biologist, is to understand why non-biologists (and in this context I class most agricultural scientists as non-biologists) cannot understand the simplest of truths. The problem of sustainability is one of numbers. The more human beings there are, the harder it is to feed them, and the more likely it is that the effort of feeding them will ruin the future for those who survive. Economists (and others) are fond of talking about growth, even about sustainable development. Biologists know that there can be no such thing.[26]

All animals survive on the excess production of other living things; that is, on the interest provided by the planet's biological capital. For long-term sustainability, there must be no incursion into capital, for that reduces future interest. Ecologists use the concept of carrying capacity to indicate how many individuals a particular ecosystem can support for a long time. But they seldom worry about measuring carrying capacity accurately. Instead, they look for signs of a healthy population in an undamaged ecosystem, signs such as resilience and stability. They would not find them in modern agriculture.

Beyond carrying capacity (and no one seriously knows what the carrying capacity of the planet is for human beings) there is an ultimate limit: sunshine. Life depends on energy to keep disorder at bay, and the ultimate source of that energy is the sun. Only plants are capable of intercepting that energy and turning it into a form other living things can use; the amount of energy captured by plants is called the net primary production.

At present, human beings account for about 40% of total potential net primary productivity.[27] There is not a great deal of slack in the system. Improving the output of present-day agriculture is at best a stop gap, which may do no more than allow more people to survive to suffer in future. Real sustainability will require a different underlying ethic, a different approach to producing food, and far fewer people demanding that others feed them.

NOTES

1 Food systems have at their foundation agriculture, and though I will touch on distribution and marketing the main focus of this chapter will be agriculture.

2 Anon., *Sustainable Agriculture: a discussion paper for Council* (London, National Farmers Union, 1993).

3 1990 Food, Agriculture, Conservation and Trade Act, cited in Gabriel, C.J. (1995) 'Research in support of sustainable agriculture', *BioScience* 45: 346–351.

4 Barnett, V., Johnston, A.E., Landau, S., Payne, R.W., Welham, S.J. and Rayner, A.I., 'Sustainability – The Rothamsted Experience', in *Agricultural Sustainability: Economics, Environmental and Statistical Considerations* (eds V. Barnett, R. Payne and R. Steiner) (London, Wiley, 1995).

5 *United Nations Environment Programme Environmental Data Report 1993–94* (Oxford, Blackwell, 1993).

6 Anon., op. cit.

7 Halley, R.J. and Soffe, R.J., *Primrose McConnell's The Agricultural Notebook*, 18th edn (Oxford, Blackwell Scientific Publications, 1988).

8 Jackson, W., *New Roots for Agriculture* (Lincoln & London, University of Nebraska Press, 1985).

9 Pimentel, D. *et al.* (1995) 'Environmental and economic costs of soil erosion and conservation benefits', *Science* 267: 1117–1123.

10   I have used imperial measurements in this section as those are the original measurements of the studies in question. Conversion to SI units would not alter the conclusions.

11   Pimentel *et al.*, op. cit.

12   Evans, L.T., *Crop Evolution, Adaptation and Yield* (Cambridge, Cambridge University Press, 1993).

13   One Teragram (Tg) is 10^{12} grams, a million metric tonnes.

14   Vitousek, P.M. (1994) 'Beyond global warming: ecology and global change', *Ecology* 75: 1861–1876.

15   Evans, op. cit.

16   Vitousek, op. cit.

17   Landraces are varieties developed by farmers themselves, sometimes called folk varieties. They are generally much more diverse than breeders' varieties, and this is one quality which makes landraces valuable to certain types of farmer.

18   Fowler, C. and Mooney, P.R., *The Shattered Gene* (Cambridge, Lutterworth Press, 1991).

19   Cleveland, D.A., Soleri, D. and Smith, S.E. (1994) 'Do folk crop varieties have a role in sustainable agriculture?', *BioScience* 44: 740–751, and references therein.

20   Powledge, F. (1995) 'The food supply's safety net', *BioScience* 45: 235–243.

21   Smithson, J.B. and Lenné, J.M. (1995) 'Varietal mixtures: a viable strategy for sustainable productivity in subsistence agriculture', *Annals of Applied Biology*, in press.

22   Anon. (1995) *The Henry Doubleday Research Association's Guidelines for Organic Gardening*.

23   Cook, R.J., Gabriel, C.J., Kelman, A., Tolin, S. and Vidaver A.K. (1995) 'Research on plant disease and pest management is essential to sustainable agriculture', *BioScience* 45: 354–357.

24   Anon. (1995) 'IRRI redesigns rice plant to yield more grain,' *IRRI Reporter* 4/94: 1–2.

25   See Jackson, op. cit. and issues of *The Land Report*, a publication of The Land Institute.

26   Hardin, G., *Living Within Limits: ecology, economics and population taboos* (Oxford, Oxford University Press, 1993) provides the best exegesis of these ideas.

27   Vitousek, op. cit.

Chapter 4

Animals as food producers

Andrew Johnson

Eating people is wrong, it is generally agreed. But what about eating other animals? Only a minority of people are vegetarians: the vast majority see nothing wrong with eating meat, though many have more or less strong objections to eating the flesh of certain species, or to unnecessary cruelty to animals before they are eaten. In this chapter, I shall consider how far such dietary choices, and some related political decisions, can be justified ethically.

Some strong dietary preferences are quite simply matters of taste, both literally and metaphorically, and on these little argument is possible. Most Europeans are revolted by the idea of eating insect larvae, for example, without being familiar with the taste of either. But feelings of dislike or disgust, however strong, are no basis for ethical judgements. It is generally agreed that these latter should be justifiable by rational argument, though many different systems have been proposed for how such arguments should best be constructed.

For very many people, ethical imperatives derive their potency from supernatural sources: in a 'primitive' context, taboos on certain foods may be effectively self-justificatory, while in sophisticated religions such as Judaism or Islam, dietary rules are laid down more systematically in sacred texts which have divine authority. Religious laws are unlikely to impress non-believers, however, and they offer no way of settling disputes between those of different faiths, though it is easy to exaggerate the extent of moral conflicts between different religions or cultures. But although there is a measure of broad intercultural agreement, there are also many sharp divides, and the proper treatment of animals is an issue on which there is no general consensus.

When moral standards differ, it is tempting to retreat into relativism, and take the view that different standards are appropriate in different cultures. But while this avoids the charge of 'cultural imperialism' that can be levelled at those who insist their standards are always right and others' are wrong, if cultural differences are merely matters of custom or habit, what ethical significance can actually be attached to them? Can slavery or torture – of people or other animals – really be 'right' in one set of cultural conditions and 'wrong' in another? Besides, always following tradition offers no prospect for improvement or reform. If new circumstances arise that are not specifically covered in the moral canon, then unless further divine revelation is conveniently to hand, ethics that is rooted entirely in the authority of tradition offers no way forward.

The hope that human reason can make progress towards a better and more 'humane' morality has encouraged many philosophers to devise systems in which, on the basis of one or two self-evidently true axioms, the whole of morality can be derived and justified using logical arguments. Such ethical systems include contract theories, rights theories and consequentialist theories (such as utilitarianism).

THEORIES OF ETHICS

Contract theories of ethics are based on the idea of isolated humans in a 'state of nature' joining together in a society of their own choosing for the mutual benefit of all. What the contract involves depends partly on its author's view of human nature. According to Hobbes, man is naturally acquisitive and competitive, whereas Rousseau's social contract was born not out of fear but from a spontaneous desire for co-operation. The diversity of individuals is emphasised by the contemporary American philosopher John Rawls, who proposes that the contractors should choose principles of justice from behind a 'veil of ignorance' about their own positions, in order to avoid bias due to sex, race, or social standing.[1]

Social contract theories give a legalistic account of obligations and rights, in which the emphasis is very much on their reciprocal nature. The contractual system applies directly only to those who understand and accept the contract, so there can be no direct duties to animals; instead, they may be protected indirectly by duties to other contractors who have a 'sentimental interest' in their welfare. So I might have a duty to Mary not to ill-treat her lamb, but to the lamb itself I could have no duties whatever. Because they cannot defend their own interests in court, lambs can have no legal rights to humane treatment, any more than they could become property owners or sue for libel.

The same restrictions apply, incidentally, to infants, the insane, the unborn, and to any others who are incapable of representing themselves.

As a basis for law, contractual theories have much to recommend them, and they explain the mechanism by which legal duties can be enforced. However, they tell us nothing about how much sentimental interest we ought to feel on behalf of those whose rights they deny. John Locke argued that natural reason shows that every man has a 'right' to food and drink and such necessities, and to his own property – 'at least where there is enough, and as good, left in common for others'.[2] A hundred years later, this idea set the world alight, and with the American Declaration of Independence in 1776 and the French Declaration of the Rights of Man in 1789, the doctrine of natural rights had come of age. Rights were a powerful weapon in the abolition of slavery and the emancipation of women, as well as being claimed, more recently, for animals. Rights of this kind differ from the legal rights deriving from contracts, in that no assumption of reciprocity is needed. While it takes two to make a bargain, as a result of which each side has duties and rights, statements such as 'animals cannot be said to have duties, so it is hard to give them rights'[3] completely miss the point that the assertion of animal rights is intended to make. Would we say a human baby has no rights, on the same ground? However, it must be recognised that if the assertion of rights is not backed up by convincing arguments, it will carry no more weight than any other assertion. The first proponents of human rights had to argue long and hard for their ideas, and though concerted arguments in favour of animal rights have been produced by advocates such as Tom Regan, there is a long way to go before the concept gains general acceptance.[4] It has also to be acknowledged that as rights proliferate, the potential for conflicts between them increases. Absolute human rights have been defended in connection with absolute equality, in which case there is no reason why one person's right to life or freedom should give way to another's. Allowing a hierarchy of rights, in which they come in different strengths, may make it less easy to regard them as effective constraints against actions which infringe them: on the other hand, most people would find it difficult to accept that a chicken's or even a chimpanzee's rights could possibly be on a par with a human's.

Consequentialist theories of ethics focus less on general principles and more on the expected outcome of particular actions. At the most basic level, careful consideration of consequences may persuade one that superficially attractive courses of action are not in fact in one's best overall or longer term interests. This kind of reasoning based on self-interest is not really ethical, but appeals to prudence can often be employed as useful adjuncts to ethical arguments. For instance, the loss of potentially valuable products is often used as an argument for conservation of endangered species, and health risks are cited as reasons for avoiding factory-farmed eggs or meat.

The principle of *utility*, by which actions are judged entirely on whether or not their consequences involve a net benefit for society as a whole, was proposed by Hume as a basis for morality, and developed by Bentham, Mill and a host of more recent followers.[5] The net effects of an action are assessed by summing up its effects on all individuals in terms of good and evil, happiness and unhappiness, or pleasure and pain. Bentham famously pointed out that there was no reason why this 'utilitarian calculus' should only include human beings: 'the question is not, Can they *reason*? nor, Can they *talk*? but Can they *suffer*? Why should the law refuse its protection to any sensitive being?'[6] A modern utilitarian case for a radically pro-animal moral outlook is developed by Peter Singer in *Animal Liberation*.[7] One objection to utilitarianism is that its emphasis on ends rather than means allows the most repugnant practices (such as torture) to be justified if there is a reasonable expectation that they will produce overall social benefits.

Each of the systems just outlined gives an insight into ethics and its demands, and each provides a valuable framework for thinking about moral questions. It is probably best to regard them as tools for moral thinking, each able to help with certain parts of morality, than to choose only one theory and try to use it as an all-embracing system. In *Ethics and the Limits of Philosophy*, Bernard Williams argues that instead of basing all morality on one or two simple premises, it may be better to adopt 'a holistic type of model, in which some beliefs can be questioned, justified or adjusted while others are held constant, but there is no process by which they can all be questioned at once, or all justified in terms of (almost) nothing'.[8]

According to Williams, ethics cannot be kept in a separate compartment: ethical judgements need to be made in parallel with other intellectual judgements. Changes in scientific knowledge, for example, may justify changes in ethics to achieve a more coherent whole worldview. Present-day biological knowledge is very different from that of a few hundred years ago, and it seems very possible that new knowledge about the biology of animals will cast new light on their moral status. In particular, evolutionary and behavioural studies provide evidence of similarities between other animals and humans, and ecology demonstrates the interdependence of different species in plant and animal communities.

HUMANS AND OTHER ANIMALS

Historically, there is nothing particularly new in the idea that other species are like us in many ways.

Typical hunters and gatherers do not view the animals they hunt as in any way inferior to themselves. They are seen as mental and spiritual equals, or even superiors, capable of conscious thoughts and feelings analogous, in every respect, to those of humans.[9]

Sympathetic identification of this kind was essential for successful hunting or herding, and the kind of knowledge of animal psychology that it gives remains useful today to traditional livestock farmers. But such emotional involvement with animals can make killing them a traumatic experience, and many rituals have evolved for 'distancing' the executioners from their victims before the event, and for cleansing their guilt afterwards.[10] Intellectually, the exploitation of animals could be justified by the belief that there was a fundamental difference in kind between humans and other species, an idea that goes back at least to ancient Greece, and which was adopted as part of Christian doctrine in the Middle Ages. It achieved its most extreme expression in the seventeenth century, just as experimental science was demonstrating the clear physiological similarities between humans and other animals. According to René Descartes, animals were no more than complicated machines, while humans alone possessed minds or souls. This was interpreted to mean that animals were incapable of feeling pain: 'the cry of a beaten dog was no more evidence of the brute's suffering than was the sound of an organ proof that the instrument felt pain when struck'.[11] As Keith Thomas points out, the most powerful argument for this position was that it rationalised the way people actually treated animals.

Certainly there was no scientific basis for such a sharp divide, nor was there an overwhelming theological case for denying souls to non-human animals. But the dichotomy was eminently convenient, and it has stuck. The theory of evolution raises some difficulties about just when humans were given the souls that mark them off as unique, and latterly an increasing number of quasi-scientific arguments have been brought forward to bolster the shaky dogma of human uniqueness. Man has been described, variously, as the only animal to use tools, to use language, to cook, to engage in religion, to be 'conscious', and so on. These definitions have, however, been undermined by studies of animal behaviour by ethologists such as Konrad Lorenz and Jane Goodall, which show such innate differences are more of degree than of kind. But many farmers, theologians, scientists, meat-eaters, and probably the majority of the population at large, still cling to the idea that humans are a species altogether different from any other. Such a belief need not be an obstacle to the kindly treatment of other species: indeed, some emphasis on humans' highly developed ethical faculties may be needed to justify showing more concern for members of different species than other animals naturally do. However, if we accept any duties at all towards other species, we should not deny genuine similarities, or there will be no way we can properly assess their basic needs.

TO EAT OR NOT TO EAT?

For vegetarians – at least for those whose vegetarianism is more than health fad or pure squeamishness – the similarities between humans and other animals, and a sense of inter-species community, are enough to justify avoiding meat-eating altogether. Vegetarians differ on how far it is acceptable to eat such animal products as eggs and milk. The conditions in which caged laying hens are kept readily justify objections to battery eggs at least, but welfare arguments have less force against free-range eggs or dairy produce. Vegans often ground their abstinence from all animal products, not just meat or fish, on the more or less inevitable indirect effects of livestock keeping such as the killing at birth of most male chicks, and the consignment of surplus calves to the veal trade. Some meat-eaters shelter from rational argument by insisting on essential but unsubstantiable differences between ourselves and all other animal species. But many others argue that meat-eating is natural, essential for health, enjoyable, ecologically and economically useful, and that in any case farm animals have a better or no worse life than wild ones.

Evidence for the 'natural' diet of humans is often sought in the food habits of hunter-gatherer tribes, or of our nearest ape and monkey relations. Though it is clear that humans can adapt to a wide variety of diets, including all-meat and all-vegetable regimens, it is less clear what ethical lesson could be learnt from 'natural' human dietary preferences, even if these could be established. Not all natural behaviour is morally appropriate for civilised humans, and it could even be argued that ethics is needed precisely to keep a check on natural impulses that are socially undesirable. It seems probable that early humans ate more meat than other primates, and also that hunting by humans was responsible for the extinction of many species of large mammals during the Pleistocene era.[12] There is even some evidence that a meat-rich diet actually encourages human aggressiveness.[13] But many people will still hesitate before totally condemning flesh-eating, on the grounds that the practice is very widespread among humans, and essential to life for many other animal species.

Utilitarians can even argue that, if most farm animals lead moderately good lives, they make the world a better place than if they did not exist. The issue of whether more animals (or, more usually, people) means 'better' is a notorious philosophical problem, on which ecology may help cast some light. All living creatures require energy and nutrients, and most of the available supplies on the planet are already being used. So extra farm animals will be less likely to increase the total amount of 'biomass' than to displace other creatures by appropriating their food and energy requirements. This is especially true for pigs and chickens in developed countries, which consume large amounts of high-protein food, often made largely from fish meal. Of course, the 'lives cost lives' argument can also apply in the case of crops (e.g. wheat or soya beans) which grow on land from which wildlife is fenced out, where intruding birds may be shot, and insects and rodents poisoned, to preserve the harvest for human consumption; not to mention the possible ecological effects of pollution from fertilisers, pesticides, farm machinery and the distribution chain. And though intensive animal husbandry is ecologically undesirable, it can be argued that properly managed grazing animals make sensible use of pasture which would otherwise be unproductive in human terms.

FARM ANIMAL WELFARE

Arguments about vegetarianism show no signs of abating, but in Britain at least there is a reasonably strong consensus that deliberate cruelty to animals is wrong, and also that some attention must be paid to the welfare of farm animals beyond protecting them from active and intentional cruelty. In cultures where such feelings are so weak as to be virtually absent, constructing convincing arguments in favour of animal welfare is a difficult challenge. Education and westernisation may produce a trend towards pro-welfare sentiments (though also, very often, towards higher levels of meat consumption). But even where there is a will for better treatment of livestock, the way to achieve this is not always clear. The similarities between farm animals and human beings are not so close that it is necessarily obvious what will suit them best, and much ingenious research is devoted to finding objective ways of assessing animal welfare. The main methods used are: comparing the behaviour of domestic animals with that of their wild relatives under natural conditions; experiments in which animals choose between different environments; and physiological measurements which correlate with other symptoms of stress.[14] Abnormal growth, broken bones and recognisable diseases are also reasonably assumed to be indicators of poor welfare. It must be acknowledged that ultimately we can only assess what an animal is feeling by reference to human standards: 'it should be assumed that if a procedure is likely to cause pain in man, it will produce a similar degree of pain in other animals'.[15] We cannot be *certain* that other creatures feel pain in the same way we do, but neither, as Wittgenstein pointed out, can we be sure that other *people* feel pain as we do, merely because they use the same word.[16] Codes of practice proposed by the government-sponsored Farm Animal Welfare Council take a common-sense view of the behavioural needs of livestock, based on the so-called 'five freedoms':

- freedom from thirst, hunger or malnutrition
- freedom from discomfort
- freedom from pain, injury and disease
- freedom to display most normal patterns of behaviour
- freedom from fear, or distress

It should not be supposed that 'traditional' agriculture necessarily meant a better deal for farm animals: modern standards of nutrition and veterinary treatment have made very positive contributions to animal welfare. But the shift to labour- and space-saving systems of intensive animal husbandry often involves much closer confinement, for poultry and pigs in particular, with a consequent reduction in their freedom to 'display most normal patterns of behaviour'. The contrast between free-range chickens and those kept in battery cages is striking: the former roam around, scratch, dust-bathe, and interact with each other; while the latter appear listless and are mostly silent in their regimented rows of cages. They are so closely packed they waste little energy moving about or keeping warm, and in summer or in hot climates birds in intensive units may overheat or even suffocate. Feeding, watering and egg-collecting are all automated: even their droppings fall on to conveyor belts for automatic disposal. All this makes for economic efficiency in terms of the maximum number of eggs at the minimum price. Many breeding sows are also kept in close confinement, in stalls so narrow they cannot turn round, though this system is now being phased out in the UK. The notorious 'veal crate' has also been banned in Britain, though many calves are still exported to the continent where they live out their short lives confined in semi-darkness, being fed an iron-deficient and wholly liquid diet to ensure they produce the 'white' meat prized by gourmets. Overcrowding of animals kept in groups rather than individual cages can result in aggressive behaviour, for which drastic remedies such as dehorning or debeaking are routine solutions.[17]

The conditions in which animals are housed are only one aspect of modern farming with welfare implications. The trend towards larger numbers of animals being under the care of fewer farm workers can result in less awareness of the animals' general health and condition, and especially less care for them as individuals with different peculiarities or particular needs. Selective breeding to produce creatures which put on the maximum weight in the shortest possible time with the minimum food input can result in the animals' general welfare being seriously compromised. For example, Belgian Blue cattle have a leg muscle conformation that gives high meat yields, but means that the cows cannot calve except by Caesarean section. Chickens and turkeys raised for meat grow so fast that their legs and lungs are stressed to the limits. As a result, respiratory infections are prevalent, and birds that are too heavy to stand often suffer painful ulceration of thighs and breast from prolonged contact with faeces-soaked litter.

It is often argued that the farmer's best interests financially are served by having healthy and happy animals. However, this is only true up to a point: sickness or poor welfare are economically important only insofar as they affect the efficient conversion of feed into end product. In this respect dairy cattle are better off than battery hens, because milk yields tend to decline with poor husbandry. But the pressure to produce more and cheaper products is ever-present, and modern dairy cattle are increasingly susceptible to mastitis as selective breeding and dietary supplements are used to boost the amount of milk each cow yields. The proposed introduction of regular injections of genetically engineered growth hormone (bovine somatotrophin: BST) to further increase milk yields will subject dairy cattle to yet more stress, in a fight to reduce unit costs that is ironic in the context of a quota regime designed to curb European over-production of dairy produce.

Few farm animals spend their entire lives on the home farm, so transport, markets and slaughtering arrangements are important factors in welfare terms. As transport has become relatively cheaper and slaughtering more centralised, the distances over which live animals are moved have increased. Live exports of sheep and veal calves from Britain to other EU countries have recently been the focus of much attention. This trade amounted to some three million animals in 1993. Regulations governing journey lengths, rest points and feeding are particularly difficult to enforce where vehicles pass through several countries *en route* to their destination, and investigations by animal welfare agencies have produced numerous horror stories of suffering and death, demonstrating the gross inadequacy of EU inspection and regulation arrangements.[18] Even within the UK, rough handling at markets and slaughterhouses is a frequent cause of stress and injury. Stunning before slaughter is prescribed by the 1974 Slaughterhouse Act, but an exception is made for religious slaughter according to Jewish or Islamic tradition, in which the animals have their throats cut while fully conscious. Many members of these faiths now accept the overwhelming scientific evidence for the welfare benefits of pre-slaughter stunning, but unfortunately others have taken its recommendation by the Farm Animal Welfare Council as an attack on their religious freedom, and there has so far been little progress towards phasing out the practice of ritual slaughter. The lack of concern for animal welfare in some overseas slaughterhouses, particularly in Greece and Spain, has been used as a further argument against the live export trade.[19]

FOOD ANIMALS AND THE ENVIRONMENT

The environmental impact of intensive animal husbandry is of increasing concern. Traditional agriculture integrated livestock and crop production. Growing hay, legumes and other fodder for farm animals was part of a crop rotation cycle that sustained soil fertility and reduced erosion. These benefits of mixed farming have generally been discounted as farmers have come under increasing pressure from providers of capital to maximise their short-term profits. In a general move towards monoculture, arable farmers have switched to using more fertilisers, while an increasing proportion of livestock are kept in intensive systems that involve the import of much of the required feed from off the farm. The number of animals kept has been increasing world-wide, with global meat production nearly quadrupling since 1950.[20] Around 40% of world grain production is fed to livestock, and animal fodder for export is an important cash crop for many of the poorest countries. This can divert resources that could better be used to feed the population at home, as well as often resulting in soil impoverishment and erosion. Laying hens and farmed fish both need high protein diets, normally provided by feed containing fish meal. It has been estimated that 30% of the world's fish catch is converted into fish meal, wasting a limited and dwindling natural food resource.[21]

As wheat and livestock production have concentrated in different localities, straw that could have provided comfortable bedding before being converted into useful manure now often has to be ploughed in because it is uneconomical to transport it. Housing cattle on concrete or slats, and handling their faeces and urine as slurry, is also less labour intensive than using straw bedding, but because slurry cannot be spread if the ground is too wet it has to be stored in tanks or lagoons, and pollution incidents are common. Intensive pig and poultry farms seldom have sufficient land of their own to absorb the waste they produce, and its disposal can become a serious problem. This has particularly been the case in the Netherlands, where livestock densities are the highest in Europe. In 1987, 'manure laws' were introduced forbidding expansion or new development of intensive livestock farms, but these have not solved the long-term problems of excessive accumulation of minerals in soil and ground water, and gaseous emissions causing local nuisance and contributing to acid rain damage to buildings and woodlands.[22]

Extensive livestock production is responsible for a different set of environmental problems. Many of the world's rangelands, which cover a third of the planet, are degraded by proliferating weeds, soil impoverishment and erosion. Misguided development policies of settlement and irrigation have frequently exacerbated these problems, and the fencing of rangeland effectively starves out a proportion of native wild animals, as well as possibly interfering with their long-range migratory movements. The introduction of exotic 'improved' breeds to replace traditional local varieties of farm animals is often misguided, and can result in the loss of valuable genetic traits such as resistance to endemic diseases.[23] Biodiversity is threatened on a greater scale by the clearance of native forests to provide pasture land. Between 1970 and 1990, more than 20 million hectares of Latin American tropical forests were converted to cattle pasture, most of which becomes rapidly degraded and is abandoned within ten years of cutting.[24] As well as containing half the earth's species of plant and animal life, the rainforests are important as sinks for carbon dioxide, so their loss contributes to the process of global warming.

KILLING FOR PLEASURE

Advocates of hunting, shooting and fishing can argue that killing wild animals causes none of the welfare problems involved in confining farm livestock in captivity, taking them to market, etc., and that it is at least as likely as agricultural husbandry to be ecologically sustainable. They can point to the need to 'control' certain species, and to the interest in conservation shown by many people involved with field sports, notwithstanding the continuing persecution by gamekeepers of unwanted animals as 'vermin'. Against these arguments must be set the possibility of a painful and protracted death for the quarry, and the welfare implications of killing animals that have lifelong mates, or young which need feeding. In addition, the belief that people who enjoy hunting or fishing do so because they enjoy dominating and inflicting pain is often used to support an argument that field sports are morally repugnant and should be banned.

Scientific evidence confirms that prey which are pursued will experience stress and fear, and that fish, as well as warm-blooded animals, feel pain.[25] Advocates of hunting and fishing could claim that some compensation is offered by the animal's chance to escape. A clean shot of sufficient power may be a relatively painless way of killing, but many birds and beasts are wounded rather than killed outright. However, taking into account the routine suffering of farm animals, and the wild freedom enjoyed by 'game' animals prior to their demise, it may be that the actual harm done by field sports is sometimes exaggerated, and that the vehemence with which they are condemned by their opponents is an expression of moral outrage at their participants' *enjoyment* of such activities.

EATING FOR PLEASURE

This outrage fits in with a general view that people's motives and feelings colour the moral quality of their actions. Positive, good actions are better if they are done gladly and willingly, while negative and bad ones seem less so if they are done with regret. Conversely, if people really enjoy veal, as Fiddes suggests, *because* of the extreme subjugation of veal calves, this aggravates the wrong of eating meat from such a cruel system.[26] But taken to extremes, this view becomes less tenable. If lives really cost lives, eating anything at all will cause some suffering somewhere. Should all eating therefore be accompanied by gloom and guilt, in the spirit of Plutarch's remark, 'Let us eat flesh, but only for hunger not for wantonness'?[27] Or do we, perhaps, 'owe it to the plants and animals on which we live to eat them with gratitude and joy'?[28]

If there is any truth at all in the latter point of view, and food is a source of pleasure as well as of protein, the utilitarian calculus will legitimately be influenced by the gastronomic quality of the food we eat. This is not to argue that it should be an overriding consideration, or that the flavour of *foie gras*, for example, justifies nailing geese to the floor by their feet and stuffing grain down their throats through a funnel. But quality of flavour is, in general, more likely to be achieved through traditional 'organic' livestock rearing and paying attention to animal welfare.[29] Treating flesh food as a luxury, to be eaten occasionally 'with gratitude and joy' rather than at every meal, might mean putting more emphasis on taste and less on price, and so relieve some of the economic pressures that encourage excessively intensive livestock husbandry.

PROSPECTS FOR PROGRESS

At the end of the day, different people will draw the line in different places: vegans and vegetarians at one end of the spectrum, and veal and *foie gras* fanciers at the other. For anyone who takes an ethical interest in what they eat, though, reasoned decisions depend on proper knowledge of the facts. A minimum requirement, which legislation can help to fulfil, is accurate and informative labelling. Though the supermarket chains have made some commendable efforts to introduce and promote 'organic' and 'welfare' products, battery eggs are still often packed in boxes adorned by bucolic farmyard scenes obviously intended to reassure consumers. It is all too easy to accept such reassurance, particularly when free-range eggs are so much more expensive, and for this reason labelling is not the whole answer. Legislation is also needed, to set appropriate minimum standards of husbandry and to outlaw unacceptable practices. Some progress in this direction has been made in the UK with the banning of veal crates and the commitment to phase out dry-sow stalls.

Legislation for improved welfare standards that applies only to one country can easily result in the problem being exported, as has happened with veal calves, or in the exposure of farmers to unfair competition from imports produced in countries with worse standards. The rules of the European Union and the General Agreement on Tariffs and Trade make it difficult for individual countries to take a lead in such matters, as they remove the option of protective tariffs against imports from inhumane or ecologically damaging systems. Reclassifying live animals as 'sentient beings', rather than merely as products, could afford them some additional protection. There is an urgent need for wider international agreement on ethical issues affecting animals and the environment. The pressure group Compassion in World Farming has recently supported the opening of a sister organisation in France and has plans to expand into other European countries. Peter Roberts, its founder, argues that the diversity of human attitudes is a barrier to progress on a European and worldwide scale: 'we now have to follow Napoleon's advice and use bigger maps if we are to achieve lasting and meaningful progress'.[30]

NOTES

1   Rawls, J., *A Theory of Justice* (Oxford, Oxford University Press, 1972).
2   Locke, J., *Essay of Civil Government* (1690).
3   As was argued by the Bishop of Birmingham during the first reading of the Animals (Scientific Procedures) Bill, 14/11/85.
4   Regan, T., *The Case for Animal Rights* (London, Routledge, 1983).
5   Hume, D., *Enquiry Concerning the Principles of Morals*, section 143 (1751). The idea can be traced back further, cf. Hutcheson, F., *Inquiry into the Original of our Ideas of Beauty and Virtue*, Treatise II, section 3 (1725).
6   Bentham, J., *Principles of Morals and Legislation* (1789) p.310.
7   Singer, P., *Animal Liberation* (London, Jonathan Cape, 1976).
8   Williams, B., *Ethics and the Limits of Philosophy*, Third impression, with amendments (London, Fontana, 1993) p.113.
9   Serpell, J., *In the Company of Animals* (Oxford, Blackwell, 1986) p.142.
10   Ibid., pp.144–170.
11   Thomas, K., *Man and the Natural World* (Harmondsworth, Penguin, 1984) pp.33–34.
12   Martin, P.S. (1966) 'Africa and Pleistocene overkill', *Nature* 212(5060): 339–342.
13   Fiddes, N., *Meat: A Natural Symbol* (London, Routledge, 1991) p.183.

14 Stamp Dawkins, M., *Animal Suffering: the science of animal welfare* (London, Chapman and Hall, 1980).
15 RSPCA, *Pain and Suffering in Experimental Animals in the United Kingdom* (Horsham, RSPCA, 1983) p.6.
16 Wittgenstein, L., *Philosophical Investigations* (Oxford, Blackwell, 1968) §281ff.
17 Johnson, A., *Factory Farming* (Oxford, Blackwell, 1991).
18 Stevenson, P., *A Far Cry from Noah* (London, Greenprint, 1994).
19 Johnson, op.cit., pp.216–218.
20 Durning, A.B. and Brough, H.B., *Taking Stock: animal farming and the environment* (Worldwatch paper 103). (Washington, D.C., Worldwatch Institute, 1991).
21 Kent, G. (1995) 'Fish for the poor: competing with chickens', *The Ecologist* 25: 48.
22 Tamminga, G. and Wijnands, J., 'Animal waste problems in the Netherlands', in Hanley, N. (ed.) *Farming and the Countryside: an economic analysis of external costs and benefits* (Wallingford, CAB International, 1991).
23 Hall, S.J.G. and Bradley, D.G. (1995) 'Conserving livestock breed biodiversity', *Trends in Ecology and Evolution* 10: 267–270.
24 Durning and Brough, op. cit., pp.25–26.
25 RSPCA, *Report of the Panel of Enquiry into Shooting and Angling* (Horsham, RSPCA, 1980).
26 Fiddes, op. cit., p.44.
27 Ibid., p.196.
28 Meyer-Abich, K.M., *Revolution for Nature: from the environment to the connatural world* (Cambridge, White Horse Press, 1993).
29 Johnson, op. cit., ch.5.
30 Roberts, P. (1994) *AgScene* Winter, 116, 15.

Chapter 5

The equation between food production, nutrition and health

Michael Crawford and Keb Ghebremeskel

THE CHANGING FOOD COMPOSITION

Modern agriculture and food processing have altered the qualitative and quantitative balance of nutrients of food consumed by Western society. But, as only 150 generations have passed since Britain emerged from the Stone Age, human physiology is still adapted to wild foods. The largest changes in food composition have occurred since the beginning of the Industrial Revolution. The change in food composition has been substantial and has happened too fast for any selective adaptation to have occurred. Moreover, these changes happened without any guidance from medicine or science and they now need to be questioned.

The public receive virtually no education in the principles of nutrition. Nutrition has rarely been taught at school or medical school, so that, with an ill-informed public, dietary changes have gone largely unchallenged. Pressure to correct errors that could be identified has had to come from non-governmental organisations.

Mediterranean countries, which have retained a close connection with traditional values in food, have the lowest mortality rates from Western diseases. However, pressure from the European Community seeks harmonisation of food and agriculture policy and it is predictable that, in consequence, the low incidence of morbidity and mortality from coronary heart disease, stroke, diabetes and breast and colon cancer of the Mediterranean countries will rise to the northern European level.

The ethical approach to these problems is adoption of a policy to equate nutrition and health. This requires that the guidelines for food production and processing be revised. Instead of food quantity, the guidelines should promote nutrient quality.

FIVE MILLION YEARS OF HUMAN EVOLUTION

Man as a hunter-gatherer lived on a diet consisting of leaves, fruits, seeds, roots, fish and shellfish, liver, kidney, entrails, muscle and other organs of wild animals.[1-4] The hunter-gatherer living today is no longer representative of the period of human evolution when a low population density enjoyed the rich diversity of fresh foods on land, in the rivers, estuaries and coastlines. Today, many such groups, like the Australian aborigine, have been displaced from these rich territories and forced on to unproductive land.[5] A view often taken of the life of the Australian aborigine is one of poverty. However, the aborigines lived in harmony with nature and, for reasons which have only recently become apparent, were able to control their population for 50,000 years. The reality is that man could not have evolved, particularly with regard to large brain size, on bad diets.[6]

A major change in nutritional ecology of man occurred about 10,000 years ago with the domestication of plants and animals.[7] Agriculturalists developed a more static way of life around the cultivation of a particular cereal grain or root crop staple. The range of different foods consumed became progressively limited.[8, 9] Agriculture, on the other hand, enabled settled cultivators to increase food production and encouraged community development.

However, as historical accounts attest, these settled communities also had to face famine due to drought, flood, frost, infestation by pests and over-cultivation with its consequent soil erosion and crop failures. Clearing forests and crop specialisation (monoculture) reduced the diversity of food further and led to a diminishing role for, and ultimately to the exclusion of, wild foods.[10]

Different peoples developed different crops. Potatoes and maize were developed in South America whilst rice became a main staple in the Far East, and plantains dominated the high rainfall regions of East and Central Africa. As population density grew, so the loss of wild foods escalated and the diversity of foods narrowed. Increasing reliance on a single staple food such as rice or plantain led to loss of essential nutrients and hence to the deficiency diseases, kwashiorkor, beri-beri, pellagra, goitre, intussusception in adults, volvulus and rickets.[11, 12] Seventy per cent of the world's blindness, which afflicts people who live in India, is related to restricted food use, which has been aggravated by population pressure over the centuries.

These diet-related disease patterns contrast sharply with the disorders common in the USA and Europe. That these differences are not due to industrialisation and economic success is testified by their relative uncommonness in Japan. Moreover, diabetes, hypertension, coronary heart diseases and cancers are not commonly seen in surviving hunter-gatherers.[13] A transition from hunter-gathering to a settled lifestyle in the Kung San resulted in a significant deterioration in haematological nutrition.[14] There is evidence both that hunter-gatherers lived on an unsaturated, low fat diet, which would also have been rich in anti-oxidants from fresh fruits, seeds, leaves and flowers,[15, 16] and that these foods would have offered protection to the hunter-gatherer from Western nutrition-related diseases.

THE BEGINNINGS OF KNOWLEDGE ON NUTRITION AND HEALTH

In the late 1880s, Christian Eijkman in the Dutch West Indies observed that chickens in which he was studying beri-beri made a remarkable recovery when he changed their diet from hospital scraps to a better diet. He traced the disease not to infection, which had been blamed, but to the use of white, polished rice. Other pioneers, Gowland Hopkins and Paul Karrer, isolated and described the chemistry and function of vitamins, whilst W.O. Atwater introduced calorimetry to study dietary energy.

At the beginning of this century, Sir Robert McCarrison demonstrated, in experiments on rats, that a wide range of diseases occurred in those dependent on foods of poor nutritional quality. The maladies he encountered in his improperly fed animals included xerophthalmia, cataract, dermatitis, otitis media, duodenal ulcer, intussusception, fetal death, preterm delivery, uterine haemorrhage, anaemia, beri-beri, distorted vertebrae and oedema: maladies which reflected those of the human population. He experimented with genetically polymorphic rats, although today scientists use genetically streamlined rats to obtain a uniform result. An important point about his work was the wide range of disorders which occurred in response to genetic variability within the population. McCarrison's message was that a 'good diet' was made up of a variety of the 'unsophisticated foods of Nature'.

The genetic profile of Americans or Europeans throws a similarly variable response to the same Western diet in the form of heart disease, breast and colon cancer, and diverticular disease. Given a different dietary deviation, a different set of diseases is expressed, as seen in the contrasts between East Africa and London, or Tokyo and

New York. Thus, the drift from the wild, unsophisticated foods to the narrower food selection patterns of recent times has taken different directions in India, Africa and Europe, and now these different continents have different nutrition-related health problems.

WORLD WAR NUTRITION INTERVENTION

By the beginning of the Second World War, most of the vitamins had been discovered and there was a good understanding of general nutrition. In September 1939, the British Government, conscious of the debilitating effects of poor food on the fighting force in the First World War, created a Ministry of Food and appointed Professor J.C. Drummond as Chief Scientific Advisor. Drummond stressed the need to provide bread of high nutritional quality and argued for an increased consumption of potatoes, fresh green vegetables, oatmeal and cheese, as well as supplying not less than a pint of milk a day to expectant and nursing mothers and children up to the age of fifteen years, and increasing the intake of vitamins A and D through cod liver oil supply and fortification of margarine.

The aim was to secure the health and efficiency of the military and to ensure that women and children were prioritised. Drummond gathered a team of nutritional scientists, economists and people from administrative backgrounds to deliver a publicity campaign and action programme, which ranged from recruitment of 'land girls' and prisoners to work on farms, to revitalisation of Britain's beehives, and to the turning of parks and gardens into grand vegetable gardens – literally 'digging for victory'. The priority was health.

Nutrition, health and economy were often found as co-partners; for example, every part of the wheat head was used to make a bread which was truly wholemeal. The variety of meats and fish eaten was widened. Strenuous efforts were made to ensure efficient transportation of food from the docks and throughout the country. The campaign was spectacularly successful and included a fall in the death rate from heart disease. This improvement in health was not due to privation because the population actually benefited from a much greater diversity of food than it might otherwise have enjoyed.

ABANDONMENT OF NUTRITION/HEALTH POLICY AND THE RISE IN NUTRITION-RELATED DISEASE

After the war, it was assumed that all the answers to nutrition and community health were known. The Ministry of Food and its work was disbanded. This is remarkable because there was an even greater call for the Ministry post-war. Whilst some foods were in short supply during the war, there was plenty to eat and the shortages of common foods often meant people ate a greater variety of food. After the end of the war, the 'lease lend' financial support from the USA came to a halt but vegetable gardens were put back to flowers and the parks to grass and rose beds. Food shortages and rationing became a serious issue.

In response to the privations, the Ministry of Agriculture, declared a target of cheap food. This meant fast growth, and emphasised quantity rather than quality. The increase in food production was aimed at filling stomachs but was without due regard to the health of the consumer and the environment. This policy was diametrically opposed to that of the scientific nutritional expertise which had seen the country through the war in better health than it had been for some time.

Cheap food was a fatal mistake. In our opinion, it was the single major cause of the progressive rise in nutrition-related diseases, such as heart disease, that occurred post-war. In the UK, mortality from heart disease rose, until Scotland recently achieved the distinction of first place in the international mortality league. In effect, the cheap food growth-driven policy led to over-production of energy-rich, nutrient-poor foods, ending in the bizarre situation of mountains of surplus food in Europe and the extraordinary policy of farmers being paid to set aside land from agricultural use.

EFFECT OF INTENSIVE MEAT PRODUCTION

The most rapid change in food composition had its beginnings with the Industrial Revolution which occurred but five generations ago. The enclosures of the seventeenth century placed livestock in fields, an act which took away the decision on what the animal wanted, or was physiologically adapted, to eat. The animal's diet was confined to what grew in the field. The natural foodstuff of cattle was soft, bushy, leafy material of lower branches of trees, sedges, herbs and grasses, which included leaves, flowers and seeds.[17] This is a mix rich in a wide range of essential nutrients, fibre and anti-oxidants, and which has a low energy density. Pasture management was designed for high protein and high energy yields.

Paradoxically, a larger number of animals on a field resulted in better weight gain. This was because the grass was maintained short by grazing, so the diet consisted of the high-energy aspect – the growing tips. As the heaviest animals fetched the best price in the markets, the stock breeders selected for weight gain. The next step was the development of high-energy feeds. Intensification of livestock escalated after World War II. Reduced exercise due to increased levels of confinement encouraged muscle loss and weight gain – and the resultant gain was animal fat. This happened despite the fact that by 1978, when the report of the first FAO/WHO conjoint Expert Consultation on Dietary Fats was published, there were already 21 national and international expert reports calling for a reduction in the consumption of animal, and similar saturated, fats to prevent increasing mortality from heart disease.

Added to the change in animal composition during the century, the use to which animal fat was put also changed. Earlier, houses were lit by tallow (beef fat) candles; and polish for boots, saddles and other leather goods was made from animal fat. Now, electricity and fossil-fuel based polishes have taken over. So, the fat that previously lit the nation's houses is now going into food.

Intensive animal production has been characterised by an increase of saturates and a decrease of polyunsaturates.[18] An increase in consumption of saturated and total fat in Western Europe and the United States and Japan,[19–23] in certain groups of South Africans,[24] and the Solomon Islands[25] is one of the main identifiable risk factors for the rise of coronary heart disease.[26–28]

The European Economic Commission brought in a regulation that intervention subsidies would apply only to carcasses with 25% or more carcass fat. A carcass with 25% fat carries about 50% lean meat with a protein content of nearly 10%. Converting these to energy units gives a 40 to 225 balance of calories from protein compared with fat. In contrast, the average reported values for wild animals of sixteen different species from East Africa was 4% fat, 75% lean and 15% protein,[29] which converts to a balance of 60 for protein and 45 for fat.

As in cattle, a significant increase in fat content and an alteration in the ratio of fatty acids is evident in other domestic species. A pig fed on a high-energy diet produces a pork chop with 40–60% of its energy as fat and a ratio of polyunsaturated to saturated fatty acids (P:S) of only 0.2:1. The corresponding values for the wild pig would less than 20%

of the energy as fat and a P:S ratio of 2:1.[30] Selective breeding, 'improved nutritional management', confined movement, and castration in the case of beef animals, have resulted in a considerable increase in the output of animal products such as milk, beef, eggs and chicken and also of animal fat. In the past, it would have taken over six years for a steer to reach 500 kg body weight, but with feeding of high-protein and -energy feed less than 20 months is required to attain the same body weight. A 2 kg broiler is now produced in six to seven weeks instead of about fourteen weeks. Similarly, a dairy cow now produces about 9000 kg of milk a year as compared with 2000 kg about 40 years ago.

Traditionally, chicken was low in fat. The Royal College of Physicians in its 1976 report advised people to eat chicken in preference to red meat. Today, their advice would be inappropriate. At the end of the last century the carcass fat on chicken was only 2.4% but due to intensive feeding it increased to 8% by 1970; a broiler chicken has 20% or more. The same calculation as with the beef carcass again shows that more dietary energy is being delivered from broiler chicken fat than from protein.

There was also a parallel change in fatty acid composition in broiler chicken, manifested in an increase of saturated and mono-unsaturated, and a decrease in essential fatty acids. Surplus beef tallow was added to broiler chicken feeds on the grounds that it had a high energy efficiency for weight gain. Again this meant 'fat gain' and a change in the fat composition away from its natural unsaturated status towards a saturated fat.[31]

Added to the existing growth promoters, industry has been attempting to persuade Europe to use bovine somatotrophin (BST) to increase milk yields. As milk fat filled one of Europe's surplus food mountains and the Department of Health, amongst other responsible bodies, recommends that the population eats less of this type of saturated fat, it is difficult to see how the pressure to sell BST to the farmers has a connection with human needs or health. Also, BST must increase the drain on nutrient stores of the cow, so it is hard to see how it can be anything but a disbenefit to the welfare of the cow itself.

A FUNDAMENTAL ERROR IN ANIMAL FEEDING AND BSE

Over the last two decades, an increased amount of meat meal – dried and ground animal carcass – was fed to beef and dairy cattle. The use of animal products in animal feed accelerated in the early 1980s when the price of soya protein rose. This action flouted the basic ecology of livestock: herbivores were increasingly fed high protein, animal products, as though they were carnivores. This appears to have been the cause of the recent epidemic of BSE (bovine spongiform encephalopathy) in cattle in the UK.

This flawed policy introduced another elementary mistake. Grass and green leaves are the primary source of vitamin E and alpha-linolenic acid, one of the two essential fatty acids. Alpha-linolenic acid in lower animals is the precursor for eicosapentaenoic and docosahexaenoic acids. Both are involved in regulating immune system function, and docosahexaenoic acid is a major structural component of the brain.[32] Diets deficient of alpha-linolenic acid result in brain disorders. In the chicken, diets deficient in vitamin E and alpha-linolenic acid result in severe cerebellar damage called 'crazy chick disease'.

Animals not susceptible to allergic encephalomyelitis can be made so by being fed diets deficient in essential fatty acids, particularly alpha-linolenic acid, and increased protein intake makes this worse. Deficiencies of this kind undermine the integrity of the brain and its blood vessels, weaken the blood–brain barrier and that alone can increase susceptibility to viral attack.[33]

Such conditions may well have precipitated the notorious BSE crisis in the UK. On 20 March 1996, the Secretary of State for Health announced that the occurrence of ten anomalous cases of Creutzfeld Jakob Disease (CJD) in humans, in a previously unrecognised pattern, had led its Spongiform Encephalopathy Advisory Committee (SEAC) to suggest a link with consumption of brain and spinal tissue from BSE-infected cattle.[34] This led to a significant loss of consumer confidence in beef throughout the EU and to a world-wide ban on the export on British beef,[35] which had serious repercussions for Britain's relations with other EU states.

LIVER VITAMIN A AND TERATOGENIC RISK

A similar mistake was made with feeding vitamin A as a growth promoter to livestock. Vitamin A is an unnatural constituent of the diet of herbivores: they would only have access to carotenoids, mainly alpha and beta carotenes. As vitamin A is part of the carnivorous food chain, bypassing the natural order has resulted in the accumulation of high concentrations of vitamin A in the liver. The Department of

Health was forced to make a recommendation that pregnant women should not eat liver because of the hazardous levels of vitamin A and the teratogenic threat presented.

However, if liver is avoided other problems can be foreseen because it is one of the best sources of B vitamins and of bioavailable iron needed during pregnancy. Moreover, a reduced level of vitamin A in the blood of newborn babies is associated with low birthweight.[36-39]

WATER IN MEAT

A new concept of 'added value' in the 1960s was the use of polyphosphates (assigned the 'E' number E450 in the EU). Phosphates are added to meat to retain water, which is beneficial for storage and cooking. With this exception, phosphates also increase the weight by adding water – so water is sold at the price of meat but dilutes the nutrient content of the product. In fairness, recent history is not all bad news. The growing recognition that synthetic colouring and flavour chemicals were hazardous, and in some cases carcinogenic, led to their replacement by plant colouring components. Squash drink manufacturers added fresh fruit juice and yoghurt processors added real fruit to their products. The net effect, however, has been to reduce nutrient content per unit of weight.

FISH AND SEA FOODS

Fifty per cent of the English income in Elizabethan times came from fish, but now pollution from industry, intensive farming methods and domestic sources has destroyed much estuarine marine life. The estuaries from prehistory are the place where the marine food chain takes off in earnest. Today, PCBs (polychlorinated biphenyls) are found in cod caught in the mid-Atlantic and fishing stocks have been decimated around the coast, in the Baltic and Atlantic.

There is now a good body of evidence to show that community health has suffered from the reduction of fish consumption and there is agreement that an increased use of sea foods, and especially oily fish, would do much to ameliorate current rates of Western nutrition-related diseases.

Fish farming on a commercial scale is a recent development. Nevertheless, its impact on the qualitative and quantitative composition of fish is apparent. Farmed fish have a higher fat content than those of the wild of the same species; some differences in fatty acids composition are also evident.[40, 41] The nature of the fatty acids is also significantly different in cultured and wild fish.[42]

PLANT PRODUCTION, PROCESSING AND NUTRIENTS

A similar process can be seen with cereals. Genetic selection for the white flour in wheat, purification of carbohydrates and sugar, the introduction of margarines and other saturated-type fats – all these meant that there was a progressive dilution of the nutrient density in the food by the increase in purified carbohydrates, sugar and fats. Through selective breeding, wider use of chemicals and processing has resulted in an increased yield of starch and an associated loss of fibre. The high incidence of diverticular disease and colon cancer in Western countries is thought to be due to the loss of fibre in the diet. As with intensive animal rearing, the consequence of injudicious, mainly market-oriented, manipulation of cereals has been ill-health.[43–46]

Most whole grains provide energy, protein, fibre, an adequate supply of B vitamins and appreciable amounts of calcium and iron. Cereal extraction (processing) removes a substantial proportion of essential nutrients. Stone-mill ground flour will contain the essential fatty acids, vitamin E, vitamin B from the germ and about 3% of fibre. The replacement of stone-mills with metal-roller mills, and the removal of the germ, pericarp and testa, has meant that vitamins E and B, most of the fibre, and a significant amount of calcium, phosphorus, iron and zinc are removed from the flour.

SUGAR

About 300 years ago, cane sugar was imported into Europe as part of the spice trade and was used by a select few as a condiment. With advances in processing techniques, a large quantity of cheap, preservable pure sugar has become widely available. A century ago the consumption of total sugar, fat and crude fibre in Britain was about 35, 75 and 8–20 g/person/day respectively. The corresponding current values are 120, 90 and 3–13. Consequently, sugar is now displacing nutritious foods, and is contributing significantly to the daily energy intake in developed countries.

FERTILISERS

The use of organic materials derived from animals and plants on cultivated soils dates back to the beginning of agriculture. Mineral fertilisers, mainly inorganic chemicals, were only introduced in the mid-nineteenth century. They were initially used as an adjunct to compost and animal manures (organic fertilisers). Since 1945 there has been an exponential increase in the use of pure mineral fertilisers; and they have now essentially replaced organic fertilisers in developed countries. Concern is being expressed that fertilisation with nitrogen, potassium and phosphorus will deplete the soil of trace elements and upset the balance of minerals, organic matter and soil quality.[47] In a long-term field experiment where only mineral fertilisers have been used, deterioration of soil structure and declines in organic content and crop yield have been reported.[48] Under the impact of heavy use of inorganic nitrogen fertiliser, the nitrogen-fixing bacteria originally living in the soil may not survive and can mutate into non-fixing forms.[49]

FATS AND OILS

Following the Industrial Revolution, butter was used sparingly by the rich: it was too expensive for the working class poor. In the nineteenth century, chemists were able to make margarine as a cheap substitute for butter from beef fat (tallow). Soon, there was an insufficient supply of animal fat to meet the demand and this led to the introduction of hydrogenation techniques which made it possible to utilise vegetable, fish and whale oils. These oils are naturally high in essential polyunsaturated fatty acids, especially those of the omega-3 variety, which protect against heart disease. Hydrogenation destroys the omega-3 fatty acids, so the net effect of the processing is to increase the consumption of saturated fat and decrease the omega-3 fats. It also introduced trans fatty acids that were not found naturally in the original oils.[50, 51] This development added a huge bolus of fat to the Western diet.

INFANT FOODS NUTRIENT COMPOSITION

Breast milk has evolved to suit the biochemical and physiological requirements of the human infant. If produced in sufficient quantity from a well-nourished mother, it satisfies the qualitative and quantitative nutrient requirements for infant growth and development during a crucial period of life. Following the widespread adoption of artificial infant feeding during the latter half of this century, there was a progressive decline in breastfeeding in the industrialised countries. In Britain and some other countries, the decline was reversed in the late 1960s: and by 1990 nearly 50% of British mothers breastfed their babies at six weeks and 25% at four months.[52] However, at the time of writing, the UK has one of the worst records, with perhaps only 30% of mothers breastfeeding to three months. The corresponding figures for New Zealand, Norway and Sweden are greater than 70% breastfeeding for six months. None of the manufacturers has successfully simulated breast milk, particularly with respect to the essential long-chain fatty acids and immuno-chemical properties.[53, 54]

The human brain is unique. Sixty per cent of the dietary energy that an infant receives from its mother goes into brain development, and the brain is itself 60% lipid. The construction and function of that lipid requires long-chain polyunsaturated fatty acids (LCPs) to build the brain. Human milk contains LCPs, and in 1978 there was enough evidence for an FAO/WHO Committee[55] to state that LCPs should be included in formulae. However, the formula companies resisted this recommendation.

There is now evidence from infant mortality studies that babies previously fed on formula had reduced brain cortical levels of docosahexaenoic acid (DHA),[56] while preterm and term infants fed formulae perform less well in cognitive and visual tests compared with those fed on human milk.[57–59] Supplementing the formula with DHA improved performance. Follow-up studies of preterm babies showed that at eight years of age, those fed formula had an 8 point IQ deficit compared with those fed human milk.[60] A comparison made at nine years of age found that term babies fed formula had significantly more mild central nervous system disabilities than those who had previously been fed their mother's milk.[61] It is not the role of scientists to justify further the presence of LCPs in human milk. If the formula companies wish to continue to leave them out, it is up to them to justify their omission.

DIETARY TRENDS IN DEVELOPING COUNTRIES

Are the developing countries immune from these degenerative diseases? From initial indications the answer is unfortunately 'no'.

A number of high, medium and even low-income countries are duplicating the agricultural production and food processing practices of Western countries without appraisal of the health implications.

Many of the high and medium income countries import processed foods, beef and chicken from Europe and the USA for consumption. Nowadays, it is also common to see cattle of European breeds being intensively fed on cereals for beef and milk production in many countries of Africa, the Middle East, Asia and South America and broiler chicken production is now a norm. Sugar-loaded soft drinks and fast foods are now well-established and highly regarded in various developing countries. Perhaps most noticeable is the speed with which the dietary habits and lifestyle of the West are being fostered and accepted, particularly by urban elites. In a number of developing countries, breastfeeding has declined considerably and is regarded as a social taboo by many, including some educated mothers.

Traditionally, people in the Middle East depended on cereals (wheat, barley, rice, maize), legumes (broad beans, lentils, chick peas), dates and fish. Much bread was consumed and lean meat was eaten rarely. Cereals and starchy roots supplied over 70% of calories and 68% of protein in 1966, while average daily animal protein consumption was only 13 g.[62]

The transformation in nutritional habits in the industrialising countries may best be illustrated by Saudi Arabia. In 1966, per capita consumption of meat was 48 g; of sugar and sweets, 29 g; of cereals, starch roots, pulses and seeds, 375 g; of vegetables and fruits, 500 g; and energy and protein intake were 1830 calories and 49 g, respectively. Cereals accounted for 60% of the calories and 60% of the protein, and the consumption of animal protein was only 12 g. These figures are comparable to those of subsistence agriculturalists, who would derive about 60–75% of energy from starch, 10–15% from protein, 10–15% from fat and about 5% from refined sugar. Currently, however, the nutrient consumption of urbanised Saudi society is qualitatively and quantitatively similar to that of the affluent societies of the West. The food consumed is likely to be high in calories, with over 40% derived from fat, about 20% from refined sugar, over 15% from protein and about 25% from starch. Moreover, it will be low in fibre and in the essential omega-3 fatty acids.

The outcome of the dietary changes is being manifested in a significant rise in the frequency of 'affluence diseases' (Western diseases) among the educated elites and other prosperous groups, particularly in the cities of developing countries. Cardiovascular diseases, high blood pressure, diabetes, dental decay and appendicitis are now common in the adult population in the Caribbean, Brazil, the Philippines, Mexico, India, the Middle East and in many cities of Africa, Asia and South America. In 1987, there were 37% and 44% more admissions for diabetes and hypertension, respectively, to a Saudi hospital in Riyadh, than over the same period of time in 1983. The increase in the frequency of high blood pressure and diabetes in the urban centres of various developing countries is linked to obesity. Of the adult population in the Caribbean, about 35% of males and 50% of females are overweight. Since poverty is yet to be eradicated in these countries, the present state of health can be described as the co-existence of diseases of 'poverty' and 'affluence'.

DIETARY RECOMMENDATIONS

Various dietary recommendations designed to alleviate the problem of chronic degenerative diseases have been proposed by national organisations of developed countries and international organisations such as the WHO and the FAO. They recommend a decrease in the consumption of total fat, saturated fat, sugar and salt and an increase in the intake of fibre. It is hoped that the target can be reached by eating of more fruits, vegetables, cereals, pulses and nuts, and by eating of less refined sugar, cheese, and intensively produced meat and eggs. All these recommendations address the consumption side of the equation instead of tackling the root problem, which lies in food production and processing practices. But it is not a credible objective to implement these dietary recommendations when at the same time the agricultural and food industry is producing fat animals, removing fibre from cereals and incorporating refined fat and sugar in so many foods.

Moreover, it would be regrettable if, despite our extensive knowledge of the relationships between nutrition and health, developing countries were to import the mistakes of Western countries, at a time when attempts are being made to rectify them in the West. There is need for developing countries to acquire the considerable scientific and technical 'know how' that the Western food industry has to offer, but they should learn from our mistakes and not copy our agricultural and food policy indiscriminately.

STRATEGIES FOR CHANGE

There are several strategies to avoid falling into the trap and to lay foundations for future health.

Tradition

Traditional African, Asian, Middle Eastern, as well as European, foods are nutritionally superior to modern Western foods, if consumed in sufficient amount. Consequently, the way forward is to foster and improve traditional food supplies.

Food and nutrition policy

A credible and integrated policy on food, agriculture and health must be developed internationally. The targets for food should focus on nutrient production.

Education

Nutritional awareness needs to be stimulated through nutrition education at all levels and backed by nutritional advice and information. This will not only involve reassessment of the direction but also the development of a new infrastructure within schools, agricultural colleges, universities, medical schools, and health service and government regulatory services.

Health policy

Nutrition during the critical periods of fetal life and infancy determines brain development, while adult diseases such as high blood pressure and obesity are also thought to be linked to this early nutrition. Therefore, nutrition, health and education policies should target mothers and their babies, school children and young women of child-bearing age.

RECOMMENDED CHANGES IN AGRICULTURAL AND FOOD POLICY

It is not possible to give an exhaustive overview of what needs to be done, although the principle is simply to make the link between food production and health. For example:

- Set aside land could be given over to extensive meat and milk production. A redesigned, diverse spectrum of plant foods for animals would provide the missing roughage and a wide range of leaves, flowers, seeds, nuts and herbs, which would give the meat improved flavour and anti-oxidant properties.
- The genetics of livestock previously selected for weight gain should be avoided, as they may well have been turned into genetically obese animals.
- The requirement for cereal crop, vegetable and animal production should be changed from weight gain to nutrient gain.
- The trace element status of soils and soil condition must be given high priority, and research needs to be done on soil micronutrients and plant nutrient value.
- River and estuarine pollution has to be brought back down to near zero.
- A new initiative needs to be taken on an integrated health/farming/food-processing policy and on rational use of the ocean's resources. We need to develop sea fish ranching, ocean and sea bed productivity, and seaweed and sea food farming.

CONCLUSION

Throughout history, the health and prosperity of populations have been altered by the food they eat.[63] The challenge is to recognise the power of the multi-generational changes induced by changing food consumption patterns. It then becomes possible to move forward with a policy to improve the health and abilities of future generations, as was envisaged and briefly achieved in Britain during the Second World War.

NOTES

1   Eaton, S.B. and Konner, M. (1985) 'Palaeolithic nutrition: a consideration of its nature and current implications', *New England Journal of Medicine* 312, 283–289.

2 Crawford, M.A. and Crawford, S.M., *What We Eat Today* (London, Neville Spearman, 1972).
3 Lee, R.B. and DeVore, I., *Kalahari Hunter-gatherers* (Cambridge, MA, Harvard University Press, 1976).
4 Simopoulos, A.P. (1991) 'Omega-3 fatty acids in health and disease and in growth and development', *American Journal of Clinical Nutrition* 54, 438–463.
5 Gebbie, D., *Reproductive Anthropology, Descent Through Women* (Chichester, John Wiley, 1982).
6 Crawford, M.A. and Marsh, D.E., *Nutrition and Evolution* (New Canaan, Keats Publishing, 1995).
7 Ucko, P.J. and Dimbleby, G.W., *The Domestication and the Exploitation of Plants and Animals* (London, Duckworth and Co. Ltd, 1969).
8 Crawford and Crawford, 1972, op. cit.
9 Jelliffe, E.F.P. and Jelliffe, D.B., 'Diet', in *Encyclopedia of Human Biology*, vol. 3, Dulbecco, R. (ed.) (San Diego, Academic Press Inc., 1991), pp.17–30.
10 Barnicot, N.A., 'Human nutrition: evolutionary perspectives', in *The Domestication and the Exploitation of Plants and Animals*, Ucko, P.J. and Dimbleby, G.W. (eds) (London, Duckworth and Co. Ltd, 1969), pp.531–545.
11 Crawford and Crawford, 1972, op. cit.
12 Barnicot, 1969, op. cit.
13 Brothwell, D.R. 'Dietary variation and the biology of early human populations', in *The Domestication and the Exploitation of Plants and Animals*, Ucko, P.J. and Dimbleby, G.W. (eds) (London, Duckworth and Co. Ltd, 1969), pp.531–545.
14 Fernandes-Costa, F., Marshall, J., Ritchie, C., van Tonder S.V., Dunn-David, S., Jenkins T. and Metz J. (1984) 'Transition from a hunter-gatherer to a settled lifestyle in the Kung San: effect on iron, folate, and vitamin B_{10} nutrition', *American Journal of Clinical Nutrition* 40, 1295–1303.
15 Leaf, A. and Weber, P.C. (1987) 'A new era for science in nutrition', *American Journal of Clinical Nutrition* 45, 1048–1053.
16 Crawford, M.A., Doyle, W., Drury, P., Ghebremeskel, K., Harbige, L., Leyton, J. and Williams G. (1988) 'The food chain for n-6 and n-3 fatty acid', in *Proceedings of NATO Advanced Workshop on Dietary w3 and w6 Fatty Acids. Biological Effects and Nutritional Essentiality*, Galli, C. and Simopoulos, A.P. (eds) (New York, Plenum Press), pp.5–19.
17 Crawford and Crawford, 1972, op. cit.
18 Crawford and Crawford, 1972, op. cit.
19 Leaf and Weber, 1987, op. cit.
20 Crawford *et al.*, 1988, op. cit.
21 Friend, B., Page, L. and Martson, R., 'Food consumption patterns in the United States', in *Nutrition, Lipids and Coronary Heart Disease*, Levy, R., Rifkind, B., Dennis, B. and Ernst, N. (eds) (New York, Raven Press, 1979), pp.489–522.
22 Mariani-Constantini, A. (1983) 'Dietary trend in Western Europe', *Preventive Medicine* 12, 218–221.

23 Kimura, N. (1983) 'Changing patterns of coronary heart disease, stroke and nutrient intake in Japan', *Preventive Medicine*, 12, 222–227.
24 Albertse, E.C., 'Westernization and nutrition-related diseases among women in South Africa', in *Diet and Life Style, New Technology*, Moyat, E.F. (ed.) (Paris, John Libbey Eurotext Ltd, 1988), pp.25–31.
25 Eason, R.J., Pada, J., Wallace, R., Henry, A. and Thornton, R. (1987) 'Changing patterns of hypertension, diabetes, obesity and diet among Melanesians and Micronesians in the Solomon Islands', *Medical Journal of Australia* 146, 465–473.
26 Byington, R., Dyer, A.R., Garside, D. *et al.*, 'Recent trends of major coronary risk factors and CHD mortality in the United States and the industrialised countries', in *Proceedings of the conference on the decline in coronary heart disease mortality* (Bethesda, National Institute of Health, 1979).
27 Connor, W.E. and Connor, S.L. (eds), 'The dietary prevention and treatment of coronary heart disease' in *Coronary Heart Disease* (Philadelphia, J.B. Lippincott, 1984).
28 Gordon, T., Kagan, A., Garcia-Palmieri, M., Kannel, W.B., Zukei, W.J., Tillotson, J., Sortie, P. and Hjortland, M. (1981) 'Diet and its relation to coronary heart disease in three populations', *Circulation* 63, 500–515.
29 Ledger, H.P., 'Body composition as a basis for a comparative study of some East African mammals', in Comparative Nutrition of Wild Animals, *Symposia of the Zoological Society of London* 21, 289–310 (London, Academic Press, 1968).
30 Crawford, M.A., Gale, M.M., Woodford, M.H. and Casperd, N.M. (1970) 'Comparative studies on fatty acid composition of wild and domestic meats', *International Journal of Biochemistry* 1, 295–305.
31 Simoupoulos, A.P. and Salem Jr, N. (1989) 'N-3 fatty acids in eggs from range-fed Greek chickens', *New England Journal of Medicine*, 321, 1412.
32 Crawford, M.A. and Sinclair, A.J., 'Nutritional influences in the evolution of the mammalian brain', in *Lipids, Malnutrition and the Developing Brain*, Elliot, K. and Knight, J. (eds), A Ciba Foundation Symposium (Amsterdam, Elsevier, 1972) 267–292.
33 Crawford, M.A., Budowski, P., Drury, P., Ghebremeskel, K., Harbige, M., Leighfield, M., Phylactos, A. and Williams, G. (1991) 'The nutritional contribution to Bovine Spongiform Encephalopathy', *Nutrition and Health* 7, 61–68.
34 Dorrell, Stephen, Department of Health. House of Commons Statement on 20 March 1996, 'CJD and Public Health'.
35 'Mad(e) in Britain', *The Economist*, 30 March 1996, p.17.
36 Neel, N.R. and Alvarez, J.O. (1990) 'Chronic fetal malnutrition and vitamin A in cord serum', *European Journal of Clinical Nutrition* 44, 207–212.
37 Yassai, M.B. and Malek, F. (1989) 'Newborns vitamin A in relation to age and birth weight', *Journal of Tropical Paediatrics* 35, 247–249.
38 Shah, R.S. and Rajalakshmi, R. (1984) 'Vitamin A status of the newborn in relation to gestational age, body weight and maternal nutritional status', *American Journal of Clinical Nutrition* 40, 794–800.

39   Ghebremeskel, K., Burns, L., Burden, T.J., Costeloe, K., Powell, J.J. and
      Crawford, M.A. (1994) 'Vitamin A and related essential nutrients in cord
      blood: relationships with anthropometeric measurements at birth', *Early
      Human Development* 39, 177–188.
40   Nettleton, J.A. and Exler, J. (1992) 'Nutrients of wild and farmed fish and
      shellfish', *Journal of Food Science* 57, 257–260.
41   Suzuki, H., Okazaki, K., Hayakawa, S., Wada, S. and Tamura, S. (1988)
      'The influence of commercial dietary fatty acids on polyunsaturated
      fatty acids of cultured freshwater fish and comparison with those of wild
      fish of the same species', *Journal of Agricultural and Food Chemistry* 34,
      58–60.
42   van Vlier, T. and Katan, M.B. (1990) 'Lower rate of n-3 to n-6 fatty acids
      in cultured than in wild fish', *Nutrition* 51, 1–2.
43   Burkitt, D.P., 'Some diseases related to fibre-depleted diets', in *The Man/
      Food Equation*, Steele, E. and Bourne, A. (eds) (London, Academic
      Press, 1975) pp.247–256.
44   Cummings, J., 'Cancer of the large bowel', in *Dietary Fibre, Fibre-
      depleted Foods and Disease*, Trowell, H., Burkitt, D. and Heaton, K.
      (eds) (London, Academic Press, 1985) pp.161–189.
45   Cleave, T.L. and Campbell, G.D., *Diabetes Coronary Thrombosis and
      Saccharine Disease* (Bristol, John Wright, 1969).
46   Painter, N.S., 'Dietary deficiency and diseases with special reference to
      diverticular disease of the colon', in *The Man/Food Equation*, Steele, E.
      and Bourne, A. (eds) (London, Academic Press, 1975) pp.257–273.
47   Welborn, B., 'Soil life with hydrosorb: an efficient, effective organic
      fertilizer and soil builder with unique water holding capacity', in *Organic
      Materials and Soil Productivity in the Near East* (Rome, FAO, 1985)
      pp.149–159.
48   FAO (1985) 'Organic materials and soil productivity in the Near East',
      Soils Bulletin 45, 2 (Rome, FAO).
49   Welborn, 1982, op. cit.
50   FAO/WHO (1978) Conjoint Expert Consultation: *The Role of Dietary
      Fats and Oils in Human Nutrition* (Rome, FAO).
51   FAO/WHO (1995) Conjoint Expert Consultation: *The Role of Dietary
      Fats and Oils in Human Nutrition* (Rome, FAO).
52   White, A., Freeth, S. and O'Brien, M. (OPCS) *Infant Feeding 1990*
      (London, HMSO, 1992).
53   FAO/WHO, 1978, op. cit.
54   FAO/WHO, 1995, op. cit.
55   FAO/WHO, 1978, op. cit.
56   Farquharson, J., Cockburn, F., Patrick, A.W., Jamieson, E. and Logan,
      R.W. (1993) 'Infant cerebral cortex phospholipid fatty-acid composition
      and diet', *Lancet* 40, 810–813.
57   Carlson, S.E. *et al.* (1993) 'Visual acuity development in healthy preterm
      infants: effect of marine oil supplementation', *American Journal of
      Clinical Nutrition* 58, 35–42.
58   Birch, E.E. *et al.* (1993) 'Dietary essential fatty acid supply and visual
      acuity development', *Investigative Ophthalmological Visual Science* 30,
      33–38.

59 Makrides, M., Neuman, M., Simmer, K., Pater, J. and Gibson, R. (1995) 'Are long chain polyunsaturated fatty acids essential nutrients in infancy?', *Lancet* 345, 1463–1468.

60 Lucas, A., Morley, R., Cole, T.J., Lister, G. and Leeson-Payne, C. (1992) 'Breast milk and subsequent intelligence quotient in children born preterm', *Lancet* 339, 261–264.

61 Lanting, C.I., Fidler, V., Huisman, B.C.L. and Boersma, E.R. (1994) 'Neurological differences between 9-year-old children fed breast-milk or formula as babies', *Lancet* 344, 1319–1322.

62 McLaren, D.S. and Pellett, P.L., 'Nutrition in the Middle East', in *World Review of Nutrition and Dietetics*, Bourne, G.H. (ed.) (London, Pitman Medical and Scientific Publishers, 1970), pp.44–222.

63 Floud, R., Wachter, K. and Gregory, A., *Health, Height and History: comparative studies in population, economy and society in past time* (Cambridge, Cambridge University Press, 1990).

Chapter 6

Food safety: the ethical dimensions

Erik Millstone

An exhaustive review of all the respects in which ethical considerations intersect with issues of food safety would necessitate a monumental discussion. It would, furthermore, make dull reading and fail to engage with the objectives of this collection. The alternative adopted here is to examine the most important ways in which ethical considerations relate to food safety policy-making, its analysis and evaluation.

Policy-making institutions are not the only sites at which ethical considerations make their presence felt, but they are the ones in which competing perceptions and interests can most obviously collide. It is, moreover, on the shoulders of those who decide policy that the responsibility for reconciling competing values, interests and objectives falls. An analysis of the process of policy-making can therefore help us to highlight many of the most important ethical debates concerning food safety.

ANALYTICAL STRUCTURE

The discussion will be organised around three main questions: first, what are the ethical dimensions of food safety policy-making; second, are there bench-marks by reference to which the ethical issues can be judged; and third, how is the current policy regime to be judged by reference to those bench-marks?

The analysis of the ethical dimensions of food safety policy would be relatively easy if each of those three questions could be explored separately, or at least sequentially. For reasons that should become clear shortly, it is not possible to discuss those questions separately. While they can be posed separately, in practice it is not possible to answer any one of them without presupposing at least some limited range of answers to the others.

PRACTICAL CONTEXT

It is self-evident that human welfare requires, at the very least, an adequate supply of food of a sufficiently high standard to sustain and improve, rather than impair, health. Typically, food is obtained by consumers in the marketplace from private commercial suppliers. In order to protect public health and the interests of consumers, the governments of all industrialised countries, and almost all less developed countries, have established complex regulatory regimes to try to ensure that minimum food safety standards are maintained.

WHY REGULATE?

A small, but vocal, minority of commentators contends that free market processes and mechanisms can, by themselves, ensure that the public is protected from food-borne hazards. They argue, for example, that merchants who sell foods which are unsafe or unpleasant will readily gain an undesirable reputation, and therefore be unable to sell their wares. Unfortunately, however, the real world does not always conform to that simple model. Selling an unsafe or undesirable product does not always or necessarily have an adverse impact on a merchant's reputation. An adverse effect on consumer health may not be immediately apparent, and by the time a consumer becomes ill it may be impossible to trace the dietary components responsible. The adverse impact on a merchant's reputation is, moreover, little comfort to those people whose health suffers as a consequence of eating noxious products, especially if, for example, they succumb to fatal bacterial or chemical poisoning. In an unregulated market, it would always be possible for small producers who have justifiably gained a poor reputation to relaunch their products under a fresh brand name, thereby concealing the identity of the firm responsible. Such considerations have persuaded consumers, responsible traders and governments that a statutory regime is essential.

THE POLITICAL CONTEXT

Since the passage of the 1875 Sale of Food and Drugs Act, public policy-makers in the UK have taken responsibility for setting food safety standards. Since then the regulatory regimes have experienced periods of both turbulence and relative tranquillity. The period since 1985 has been one of the most contentious and turbulent periods, with more public debate about the politics of food safety policy than at any time this century. Policy-makers continue to be challenged by a wide range of groups, such as consumer organisations, animal welfare organisations, medical and health-based groups, third world development groups and organic food lobbies. Farmers, food manufacturers and trade groups are also critical of many aspects of food safety policy-making, and food safety policy debates are infused by competing conceptions of what is right and wrong.

The political context is, moreover, changing in a crucial respect. Traditionally, regulatory regimes have been established separately by the governments of nation-states. The liberalisation of trade policy is, however, now starting to set new limits on the freedom of action of national governments (and even the European Union) in the area of food safety policy-making, as in many others. National sovereignty and uncontested jurisdiction previously gave the governments of nation-states enormous scope for the exercise of discretion, both on the issue of which matters to regulate, and in setting their own regulatory regimes within their own borders. When the European Community (EC), now the European Union (EU), completed its internal market in 1992, the regulatory regimes of the member states were harmonised and integrated into a uniform and centralised EC/EU-wide system. Under the auspices of the General Agreement on Tariffs and Trade (GATT), a process of global harmonisation is under way which will result in the establishment of a set of global standards applying throughout the world, or at any rate in all those countries engaged in international trade in food and agricultural commodities. Rules currently being drawn up by the International Trade Organisation (ITO) will apply to all traded food products. Since the ITO is not a democratically accountable organisation, the ways in which it will deal with the ethical dimensions of policy may be difficult to discern. Some analysts have argued that in the process of harmonisation within Europe, standards of consumer protection fell to, or even below, what then prevailed as the lowest common denominator.[1] That argument has been extended analogously by those who forecast that as a global GATT-based regime is established, the tendency will be for standards to decline rather than rise.[2] There is, therefore, a risk that the shift in responsibility from national governments, at least some of which are democratically accountable, to the ITO (which is not) will intensify rather than diminish the contentious character of the debates about food safety policy.

FOUR MODELS OF THE RELATIONSHIP BETWEEN SCIENCE AND ETHICS IN FOOD SAFETY POLICY-MAKING

Food safety policy-making is, evidently, a highly contested domain. These contests focus not just on concrete empirical and practical matters but also on more abstract and philosophical issues concerning what could appropriately be termed the meta-structure of food safety policy debates. The discussion in this section focuses on such conceptual matters, and is concerned with two questions: first, how, in general terms, should the ingredients which contribute to policy-making be characterised? and second, how do those ingredients interact? For the purposes of this discussion it is assumed that the two classes of relevant materials are scientific and ethical considerations. That scientific judgements are relevant to food safety policy decisions is one of the few claims which is uncontested; the debate, however, concerns the role of ethical considerations and their relationship to science.

There are several competing models of the ways in which ethical considerations do, or could, contribute to food safety policy. For the purposes of this discussion, I shall outline just four of them. In describing and evaluating these models, however, substantive ethical issues will need to be explored, which partly accounts for the interconnectedness of the initial set of three questions.

Model I: positivistic extremism

Some people apparently believe that scientific considerations by themselves are sufficient to determine policy, and that the science upon which policy is based is itself socially and ethically neutral.[3] Since that view is most commonly articulated by people who are themselves directly involved in policy-making, and who are therefore best placed to appreciate the falsity of the model they espouse, it is difficult to be entirely confident that they all genuinely subscribe to this model. An alternative hypothesis would be that some wish to invoke the authority of science, and to conceal their own evaluative stance. In that case they would merely be articulating the model for rhetorical and political purposes to try to

foreclose certain types of challenges. Notwithstanding such cyni-
cism, evidence of the inadequacy of this positivistic mode will
emerge later in the discussion.

Model II: science and ethics both contribute to policy, but separately

Model II has its philosophical roots in orthodox scientistic empiricism, which assumes that science produces reliable and authoritative
conclusions, and that facts and values can and should be confined to
separate conceptual domains. This model is one to which many civil
servants appear genuinely to subscribe, especially those working in
regulatory institutions in the UK and the European Commission: in
that sense it constitutes one kind of orthodoxy. Model II can be found
explicitly articulated in both official documents and standard text-
books.[4]

On this model, both scientific and ethical considerations are
presumed to have, and are acknowledged as having, essential
contributions to make to policy, but they do (or should) function in
watertight compartments, completely separated from each other. If
the facts can be completely separated from all values, the scientific
community should be able to provide ethically and socially neutral
information, against the background of which policy-makers could
subsequently determine that which is to be deemed socially acceptable.

With this model, it is often supposed that scientific experts can
provide precise and reliable (if not entirely certain) knowledge of what
is, and what is not, safe. If that were so, then policy-makers would be
able readily to establish a framework of law, and a regime of
regulation, with which to ensure that food products are marketed if,
and only if, they are safe.

Model III: scientific debate is nothing but a form of social conflict

The third model is the most relativistic one, for it assumes that
scientific and ethical considerations are so thoroughly fused together
that they cannot be separated conceptually or practically. For
example, Schwartz and Thompson have adopted a 'view of politics,
technology and social choice ... in which their clear separation is
impossible. They are, rather, an entanglement: an inchoate mass'.[5]
Epistemologically, this model is rooted in a sceptical version of social
relativism. On this view, the contrast between facts and values, or

between science and ethics, is nominal rather than substantial, and is invoked primarily as a rhetorical tool in a power struggle between various institutions as they compete for social credibility.

Model IV: science and ethics are richly interconnected but nonetheless distinguishable

This fourth model, which I shall be arguing is the most realistic and useful, assumes (as against Model I) that scientific and ethical considerations both contribute to policy-making but (as opposed to Model II) that they are not two entirely separate spheres of discourse, and yet (as against Model III) that they can be both distinguished and disentangled. On this Model, it is assumed rather that scientific and ethical considerations, though analytically distinct, can and do reciprocally influence each other. The extent to which they can be distinguished and separated in practice is, on this model, presumed to be a matter for specific investigation in particular cases.

To illuminate some of the strengths and weaknesses of these four models I shall examine how they might try to deal with a particular example in food safety policy. The example concerns the artificial sweetener saccharin, the debate about its putative toxicity, and the resultant policy dilemmas.

THE CASE OF SACCHARIN

The synthetic sweetener saccharin has been on the market since a patent was granted in 1885, and there have been disagreements about its safety since at least 1890. Since the mid-1970s, the main controversy has focused on the question of whether or not saccharin is, or should be presumed to be, an actual or possible carcinogen. This issue arose because it then emerged that there was clear and consistent evidence from at least four long-term feeding studies on rats that saccharin causes bladder cancer in male rats.[6] The effect occurs at even moderate doses, especially when saccharin is administered over several generations.

Both scientists and policy-makers therefore had to confront the question of whether or not saccharin might also be a human carcinogen, in either or both sexes, and in relation to the bladder or possibly at other sites, instead or as well. Policy-making in this context was complicated by the fact that saccharin also appeared to be carcinogenic, but at a different site, in some other species of laboratory animals, while it appeared to exert no carcinogenic effects in yet others.

Problems were aggravated further by the fact that when tested on bacterial populations to establish whether or not saccharin provokes mutations in the genetic material contained in their cell nuclei, scientists found that in some bacterial populations saccharin did appear to provoke mutations, while in others it did not.[7] These considerations are important because if a compound provokes mutagenic damage to the chromosomes of an organism it might also be capable of initiating the growth of a tumour. This is because one route by which a compound can be carcinogenic is by being mutagenic, especially if it is a mutation which subsequent generations of the organism can inherit, in which case it deserves to be characterised as genotoxic. Therefore, ambiguous evidence of bacterial genotoxicity complicates any judgement which we might wish to make regarding saccharin's carcinogenicity, and more generally its acceptability. It is especially complicated because even if saccharin is not a human carcinogen we would wish to avoid it if it were 'merely' genotoxic, since we do not want dietary ingredients to damage our offspring. Even if saccharin were shown not to be genotoxic, however, this would not entail that it could not be a carcinogen, because there are innumerable non-genotoxic mechanisms which are involved in the promotion and progression of a tumour.

There is one further approach with which we can investigate the putative carcinogenicity of saccharin, and this involves using the techniques of epidemiology. The science of epidemiology studies the patterns of illness and mortality amongst what toxicologists rather ineptly refer to as 'the target species', namely, human beings. In this crucial respect, epidemiology differs from animal and bacterial studies because, notwithstanding any methodological limitations which it may have, any information provided by epidemiology refers directly to people, and does not require hugely problematic inter-species extrapolations, as is always the case when toxicologists test chemicals on rats, mice, guinea pigs and bacteria.

With epidemiology, the putative carcinogenicity of saccharin can be studied in two distinct ways. First, scientists can study a group of male bladder cancer sufferers to try to find out whether they were more or less likely than an otherwise comparable group to have consumed saccharin. Second, they can study diabetics and try to establish whether or not they have elevated rates of cancer of the bladder, since typically diabetics use more artificial sweeteners than other groups, and for most of this century that has meant consuming saccharin. Since it is well known that compounds can cause cancer at one site in one species but at a different site in other species, a failure to discover significantly higher rates of saccharin consumption amongst adult human male bladder cancer sufferers would not, however, be conclusive evidence that saccharin is not a human carcinogen. On the other hand, even if there were a higher rate of cancer among diabetics, scientists could not immediately conclude that it was artificial sweeteners, or even saccharin, which were responsible, because it might have been causally related directly to the diabetes, independently of saccharin consumption. More than 20 epidemiological studies on saccharin had been conducted by the early 1980s, but all on relatively small samples, using relatively poor control for possible confounders. While some of them found no significant correlations, a few did yield evidence of a possible link between saccharin consumption and bladder cancer.[8]

Given the uncertainties and equivocation both within and between animal feeding studies, bacterial mutagenicity tests and human epidemiology, a bold attempt was made in the early 1980s by a US National Academy of Sciences expert panel to estimate the upper and lower bounds of the hazard which saccharin might pose to the US population. They estimated that if, on average, the population of the USA were to ingest some 120 milligrammes of saccharin daily for a period of 70 years (which corresponded to the average level of consumption in the USA in the early 1980s) it was unlikely that fewer than 0.22 deaths from bladder cancer would occur throughout the entire US population over that period, while on the other hand it was unlikely that more than 1,144,000 extra deaths would be caused.[9] In other words, estimates of the potential carcinogenicity of saccharin for humans are characterised by an uncertainty range covering no less than six orders of magnitude.

The example of saccharin has been introduced here precisely because it is, in many respects, representative of the scientific uncertainties and ethical dilemmas which confront food safety policy-makers. What is unusual about saccharin is not the scale of the uncertainties, but the fact that there has been an authoritative attempt to estimate the magnitude of those uncertainties. Very similar uncertainties characterise, for example, the debates about the toxicity of the anti-oxidant BHA (butylated hydroxyanisol also known as E321) or organo-phosphate pesticides. The case of bovine spongiform encephalopathy (BSE or mad cow disease) is not dissimilar. We do not

know what the risk of spongiform encephalopathy being transferred
to humans might be, and it may well be slight, but if it were to occur
the consequences for those affected would be dire.

SACCHARIN AND THE FOUR MODELS

This section explores how adequately each of the four models is able
to cope with the example of saccharin.

Model I

The first model presumed that scientific considerations, by themselves, are uniquely sufficient to determine policy, and that ethical
considerations therefore need make no contribution. It almost goes
without saying that this model is completely useless when confronted
by the example of saccharin, or any other like it, but for completeness
the key points deserve to be spelled out. There are at least two major
shortcomings to this simplistic model, and they serve to highlight the
two main reasons why ethical considerations are essential ingredients
of policy-making.

First, in relation to saccharin and to many topics in the vast
complicated panoply of food safety issues, scientific knowledge is
incomplete, deeply contested and unreliable. Scientific information
cannot, therefore, uniquely determine policy. Confronted by uncertainties on such a monumental scale, policy-making must depend on
evaluative judgements, that is to say upon ethical considerations.
Policy-makers need to decide whether they are going to award the
benefit of the doubt to the food and beverage industries, and presume
that saccharin is safe until definitively proved to be a human
carcinogen, or whether, on the other hand, to give the benefit of the
doubt to consumers and presume that it is hazardous until proved
safe, that is to say to adopt a precautionary approach assuming that it
is better to be safe than sorry. Policy-makers receive conflicting advice
and representations from various interests, but the decision they make
is essentially one about arbitrating between those two opposing
pressures and those two competing options. Although policy-makers
rarely acknowledge the fact, in practice they frequently need to decide
which they deem to be more important: protecting public health in the
long run or protecting commercial interests in the short run.

It is important to appreciate, however, that even where there is
greater convergence of scientific evidence and opinion, and even

where toxicological conclusions are far less uncertain, evaluative considerations always have a vital role to play in food safety policy-making. Even if they knew the precise details of the relationship between exposure and risk, policy-makers would need to decide the magnitude of the risk deemed socially acceptable in the context of some presumed benefits which the use of that chemical might confer. Typically, people indicate that they would be more willing to accept a remote risk of adverse chronic effects from a food preservative which effectively inhibits the growth of dangerous bacteria than from a colouring agent which has only a cosmetic effect. Similarly, the more people believe that artificial sweeteners can help them to lose weight the more likely they are to accept a marginally increased risk of cancer, while if they came to believe the evidence which indicates that saccharin, and other artificial sweeteners, are either unhelpful or actively counter-productive in relation to weight loss, their valuations of the relationship between risks and benefits would almost certainly be transformed.[10] Those considerations are sufficient to indicate that Model I is hopelessly inadequate.

Model II

Since policy is the product of both scientific and evaluative con-siderations, the remaining dispute concerns the nature of the relation-ship between those two sorts of contributions. The example of saccharin reveals that while nominally scientific considerations can be presented as if they were entirely independent of, and prior to, any evaluative judgements, in practice, ethical and social considerations often influence both the production of scientific conclusions and their deployment in the policy process. Science is itself often, and perhaps always, dependent in complex ways on prior evaluative judgements. This is certainly so in the saccharin case. The central inadequacies of Model II can be highlighted by identifying some of the evaluative considerations which lie concealed within, or behind, specific scien-tific judgements concerning saccharin.

The conduct of toxicological inquiry and discourse is dependent, for example, on evaluative judgements about the permissibility and value of animal experimentation. However important those issues may be, they arise in many parts of biological work, and not uniquely in food safety work. Given that animal studies are part of the discipline, toxicological work requires making, implicitly or explicitly, judgements which are, at least in part, evaluative about issues such as the number of animals to be used in any particular test, the range of doses to be administered, and sometimes even the route of administration. These may be highly technical matters but that does not mean that they are socially or ethically neutral. Decisions about the numbers of animals to be used are important not just in relation to issues of animal welfare, but human welfare too. If only small groups of animals are used, the statistical tests which have to be applied to interpret the results will be relatively insensitive. Insofar as the safety tests are insensitive their incorporation into policy-making can, at best, provide only a relatively low level of consumer protection. As Sharratt has argued:

> To be 95% certain of detecting an abnormal reaction in one animal out of 20, about 60 animals are required. To have 99% certainty of detecting one abnormal reaction in 100 animals, 500 animals are required. An even larger number of animals is necessary if it is desired to detect an abnormal reaction occurring at low frequency in the population.[11]

Since long-term animal feeding tests typically involve the use of no more than 400 animals, of which only 300 are exposed to the test compound, the sensitivity of the toxicological and statistical tests is extremely limited.

One of the features of the community of professional toxicologists which seems remarkable is just how little energy they devote to the problem of estimating the extrapolative validity of their models.[12] With the honourable exception of some pioneering work by Salsburg, the silence on this matter is quite deafening.[13] Simply treating the results of animal experiments as if they were a valid basis for judgements about humans, when there is evidence indicating that such an assumption is false, implies ascribing a higher value either to the commercial interests of the food and chemical industries, and/or to the occupational interests of the toxicology profession, than to the protection of public health.

In practice, the situation is often rather worse than that. All too often official regulatory bodies, along with industrial and academic toxicologists who represent industrial firms, covertly give the benefit of the doubt to the chemical rather than to the consumer; and the saccharin case serves to illustrate this point. For example, the UK's Committee on Toxicity, the European Commission's Scientific Committee for Food and JECFA (the Joint Expert Committee on Food Additives of the World Health Organisation and the UN Food and

Agriculture Organisation) all accept the results of animal studies at face value when they imply no adverse effect, but they inflict a disproportionate scepticism upon any study in which the results imply an adverse judgement on saccharin; if they had not been doing so, saccharin would have been banned back in the 1970s. All too often, the results are interpreted in an opportunistic and biased fashion, so we are entitled to conclude that commercial interests take precedence over the protection of public health.

An important ethical judgement, therefore, which almost always passes unacknowledged, is the decision not to investigate the question of the extent to which animal studies are relevant to humans. There are no scientific or technical reasons why the research community should not extend our epidemiological knowledge and then compare the results of human studies with those from tests conducted on laboratory animals, cells and bacterial cultures. The question of the extrapolative validity of mutagenicity tests is almost always cast in terms of how well or poorly they compare with studies on animals, rather than their direct relevance to humans.[14] One reason why this is important is because if the scientific community started to estimate the extrapolative validity of their models for humans, they might learn when particular models are more or less reliable. It would, for example, be important if we learnt that the lung of the rabbit provides a better model for the human lung than do the lungs of other species. If, for example, the kidney of the rat is more relevant than the kidney of the rabbit to humans, the sooner we establish that the better, for at least two of those three species. Gaining such information would be a first step towards a programme to develop toxicological models which are demonstrably more relevant to humans than the ones currently being used. The failure to pursue such a programme of research illustrates how marginal consumer protection considerations are to commercial toxicology and to the regulatory policy-making process.

There is a powerful incentive for both government and industrial scientists to continue avoiding those issues because they are unwilling to demolish their fragile structures until they have something more robust with which to replace them. There is, furthermore, a powerful vested institutional interest in sustaining the opinion that their judgements are purely scientific, and do not rely on non-scientific considerations.

Given that toxicologists use animals in experiments, the question of how thoroughly, and in which respects, the animals should be examined involves both ethical and technical considerations. While regulators can list at length their requirements concerning the parameters upon which experimenters must report, those lists are inevitably finite and limited. It is not yet normal practice to require evidence from tests designed to establish whether or not food chemicals have oestrogenic effects, but a debate on this issue has recently become rather vigorous.[15] There are at least two pathological considerations impinging on this matter. First, the incidence of breast cancer in women has been increasing over recent decades, while the age of onset has also been declining. There is strong evidence to suggest that many breast cancers are either initiated or promoted by oestrogen-mediated processes; indeed this underlies the popularity of the drug tamoxifen, which preferentially attaches to oestrogenic receptors, and so might diminish the risk of tumour formation or proliferation.[16] Evidence has accumulated, moreover, indicating that in men the numbers and quality of sperm have declined.[17] An increasing number of scientists have been arguing that oestrogenic activity by industrial chemicals may well be responsible for at least part of that decline.[18] At the time of writing, no official regulatory body has yet modified its data requirements to include a study of oestrogenicity, but the decision on what to require, in these circumstances, is in key respects an ethical judgement.

Models III and IV

While articulating a critique of Model II, by drawing upon the example of saccharin, I have *ipso facto* disentangled precisely some of those elements which the proponents of Model III insist cannot be distinguished. I have shown how ethical and scientific considerations can and do simultaneously contribute to toxicological and regulatory judgements. It follows, therefore, that Model IV is to be preferred to Model III.

There is no particular difficulty, moreover, in distinguishing between a judgement concerning the form which an animal study should take, and the empirical results which eventually emerge from such a study. The form of the resultant data may be dependent upon those judgements, but the content of those data are not determined by either the technical or the evaluative considerations which influenced those judgements. Evaluative considerations can and do influence the interpretations which different parties will place on the subsequent results, but the results are, in an important respect, independent of those surrounding considerations. While it is almost certainly the case that data are almost always presented in an interpreted form, it does not follow that there is no such thing as uninterpreted data. At least some scientific facts are almost bound to be ethically and socially neutral, but they are typically not the ones vital to policy-making.

Therefore, Model IV is to be preferred to Models I, II and III, in part, not because scientific work can or should be conducted in an intellectual space that is devoid of values, but rather because it should be conducted with an explicit rather than a covert set of values. The fuller the account of the values adopted by scientific personnel and institutions, the more straightforward it is to appreciate the proper significance of their methods, data, interpretations and conclusions for public policy.

WHAT ARE THE BENCH-MARKS FOR EVALUATING FOOD SAFETY POLICY REGIMES?

The central ethical issue in food safety policy-making is concerned with the direction in which, and the extent to which, decision-makers should give priority to competing interests and values. Often that comes down to the question identified above, namely how to award the benefit of the many doubts which afflict the scientific evidence as between competing interests and values.

While there are, for example, differences of interest between organic farmers and non-organic farmers (and even more strikingly between organic farmers and agrochemical companies), and between farmers, on the one hand, and food processors or retailers, on the other – to a first approximation the pivotal policy-relevant divide is that between consumer interests, on the one hand, and commercial interests, on the other. It is self-evident that the commercial interests of firms in the food sector do not always coincide with those of consumers. Otherwise, policy-making would be unnecessary or uncontroversial.

The bench-marks by reference to which the food safety regulatory regimes can be evaluated are primarily those concerned with estimating the extent to which they serve the real or perceived interests of consumers, on the one hand, and those traders, on the other – in so far as they diverge. A technical innovation which allowed food manufacturers to produce wholesome foods with a decreased risk of bacterial contamination, and which otherwise introduced no new risk, would be one which should recommend itself to producers, consumers and regulators alike. The use of a compound such as BHA as an anti-oxidant to extend the shelf-life of fried snack foods, and to inhibit the biodegradability of plastic packaging materials, but with no benefits for consumers, may be very attractive to corporate interests but less so to consumers given that there is evidence that BHA causes cancers in several species of laboratory animals, and (according to some very recent evidence) might also be oestrogenic.[19]

It would be difficult to explore the entire food safety agenda, topic by topic, to establish the precise ways in which the benefit of the doubt has been, or is being, awarded. A more broadly based proxy indicator, however, recommends itself. Other things being equal, the more transparent and democratically accountable a policy-making regime is, the more likely it is to acknowledge the scientific uncertainties and conflicts of interest, and therefore it can be expected to deal more fully and honestly with ethical considerations.[20] The more secretive a policy-making system is, the less it is scrutinised, the easier it will be for a technocratic gloss to be placed on the grounds for, and outcomes of, policy-making. These considerations suggest a general set of guidelines by reference to which policy-making institutions could be reformed. Such a programme of reform should enable them to deal more honestly and effectively with both the ethical and the scientific dimensions of food safety policy, and their inter-relationships.

HOW DO FOOD SAFETY REGIMES COMPARE WITH THOSE BENCH-MARKS?

The saccharin example illustrates the general conclusion that policy-making institutions in the UK and Europe rarely acknowledge either the scientific uncertainties or the role of ethical considerations, and this is closely related to the fact that they are relatively secretive and unaccountable. In those cases where I have compared the available scientific evidence with the conclusions of British and European policy-makers, I am convinced that the interests of consumers is typically subordinated to commercial interests, even though consumer protection is the ostensible goal of the regulatory institutions.

SUMMARY AND CONCLUSION

The evidence and the ideas outlined in this chapter suggest that while a wide range of ethical considerations play an integral and indispensable role in food safety policy-making, their role is often not properly acknowledged. The main ethical dilemma facing policy-

makers is how to deal with the, all too familiar, circumstances in which
the interests of producers and consumers diverge, while the scientific
evidence is incomplete and equivocal. Many of the shortcomings in
food safety policy can be attributed to a failure to acknowledge the
limitations of scientific knowledge and/or the role of differing
evaluative considerations and judgements. Those problems are at
their most severe when policy-making institutions operate in a
relatively secretive manner and in the absence of procedures for
systematic democratic accountability. These conclusions, therefore,
have implications for public health, scientific research and political
science.

NOTES

1 Millstone, E., 'Consumer protection policies in the EC: the quality of
   food', in Freeman, C., Sharp, M. and Walker, W. (eds), *Technology and
   the Future of Europe* (London, Pinter Publishers, 1991), ch. 20.
2 Lang, T. and Hines, C., *The New Protectionism: protecting the future
   against free trade* (London, Earthscan, 1993).
3 Masood, E. (1995) 'Vote on growth hormones in meat sparks row with
   FAO', *Nature* 1, 376, 20 July, 207.
4 Ministry of Agriculture Fisheries and Food, CODEX Risk Assessment
   and Management Procedures, Paper CX/FAC 95/3 presented to the 27th
   Session of the CODEX Committee on Food Additives and Contami-
   nents of the Joint FAO/WHO Food Standards Programme, Rome, July
   1995; Ottoboni, M.A., *The Dose Makes the Poison: a plain-language
   guide to toxicology* (New York, Van Norstrand Reinhold, 1991), see e.g.
   Ch. 15 'Risk'.
5 Schwartz, M. and Thompson, M., *Divided We Stand: redefining politics,
   technology and social choice* (London, Harvester Wheatsheaf, 1990), p.1.
6 Arnold, D.L., Krewski, D. and Monroe, I.C. (1983) 'Saccharin: a
   toxicological and historical perspective', *Toxicology*, 27(3-4), 179–256,
   see esp. p.179.
7 Ibid., pp. 192–3; the issue has been explored in greater detail, but with the
   same inconclusive results in Arnold, D.L. and Boyes, B.D. (1989) 'The
   toxicological effects of saccharin in short-term genotoxicity assays',
   Mutation Research, 22, 69–132.
8 Arnold, D.L. *et al.*, op. cit., esp. pp.224–239.
9 Wilkinson, C., Proceedings of the 10th International Congress of Plant
   Protection, 1983, Vol.1, p.46; cited by Graham-Bryce, I. (1984) *Chemistry and Industry*, 17 December, p.864.
10 Rogers, P.J. and Blundell, J.E. (1993) 'Intense sweeteners and appetite',
   American Journal of Clinical Nutrition, 58, 120–121; Rogers, P.J. and
   Blundell, J.E. 'Sweet carbohydrate substitutes (intense sweeteners) and
   the control of appetite: scientific issues', in *Appetite and Body Weight
   Regulation: Sugar, Fat, and Macronutrient Substitutes*, Fernstrom, J.D.

and Miller, G.D. (eds) (Boca Ratan, Boston, CRC Press, 1994); Bellisle, F. and Perez, C. (1994) 'Low-energy substitutes for sugars and fats in the human diet: impact on nutritional regulation', *Neuroscience and Behavioral Reviews*, 18(2), 197–205.

11   Quoted by the Commission of the European Communities, 'Food Additives and the Consumer', Brussels, 1980, p.43.

12   Conning, D.M. 'New approaches to toxicology testing', in *Food Toxicology: Real or Imaginary Problems?*, Gibson, G.G. and Walker, R. (eds) (London, Taylor & Francis, 1985).

13   Salsburg, D. (1983) 'The lifetime feeding study in mice and rats – an examination of its validity as a bioassay for human carcinogens', *Fundamental and Applied Toxicology* 3, 63–67.

14   Ottoboni, M.A., *The Dose Makes the Poison: a plain-language guide to toxicology*, 2nd edn (New York, Van Norstrand Reinhold, 1991).

15   Jobling, S. *et al.* (1995) 'A variety of environmentally persistent chemicals, including some phthalate plasticizers, are weakly estrogenic', *Environmental Health Perspectives* 103(6), June, 582–587; Brotons, J.A. *et al.* 'Xenoestrogens released from lacquer coatings in food cans', *Environmental Health Perspectives* 103(6), June, 608–612.

16   Baum, M., *Breast Cancer: the facts* (Oxford, Oxford University Press, 1988); Lee Davis, D. (1993) 'Medical hypothesis: zenoestrogens as preventable causes of breast cancer', *Environmental Health Perspectives*, 101(5), 372–384.

17   Sharpe, R.M. (1993) 'Declining sperm counts in men – is there an endocrine cause?', *Journal of Endocrinology* 136, 357–360; Sharpe, R.M. and Skakkabaek, N.E. (1993) 'Are oestrogens involved in falling sperm counts and disorders of the male reproductive tract?', *Lancet* 342, 29 May, 1392–1395; Mittwoch, U. *et al.* (1993) 'Male sexual development in "a sea of oestrogen"', *Lancet* 342, 10 July.

18   Mittwoch, U. *et al.*, ibid.

19   Jobling, S. *et al.*, op. cit.

20   Millstone, E. 'Can the political role of science be democratised, and if so how?', Eduardo Goncalves, M. (ed.), *Ciencia and Democracia* (Lisbon, Portuguese Federation of Scientific Societies, forthcoming).

Chapter 7

Ethical analysis of food biotechnologies: an evaluative framework

Ben Mepham

INTRODUCTION

In 1990 the Advisory Committee on Novel Foods and Processes (ACNFP) received a submission concerning sheep modified to carry a human gene. The gene coded for Factor IX, a protein involved in blood clotting which is required in the treatment of haemophiliacs. At that stage the company involved had no interest in selling the potentially highly valuable animals carrying the human gene. However, they wished to be able to market the large majority of animals in which modification had not been accomplished.[1]

This opening paragraph of a report published by the UK Ministry of Agriculture highlights a number of issues, popularly perceived as 'ethical', which are posed by the application of modern biotechnology. In the first place, the project involved the genetic engineering of farm animals; second, it entailed the transfer into animals of human genes; and third, the application sought permission to sell meat, for human consumption, derived from animals which had been involved in an experimental genetic engineering project.

Undoubtedly, such issues touch raw nerves. According to public opinion surveys, the majority of people in the EU are opposed to biotechnologies involving farm animals, with 20% believing that such applications 'are morally unacceptable and should be banned by public law'.[2] Yet there is more to ethics than intuitive (adverse) reactions; and the impacts of modern biotechnology are of wider significance than these. Moreover, not a few people would share Glover's concern that 'By easy stages, we could move to a world which none of us would chose if we could see it as a whole from the start'.[3] If society is to come to sound ethical judgements on the regulation of such revolutionary technologies, a measured, rational approach is called for. What is required is a means of examining the pros and cons of biotechnology in a way which will facilitate ethically acceptable public policy decisions on what should be allowed, regulated or proscribed.

The aim of this chapter is to consider the range of ethical issues raised by biotechnology applied to food and to explore means of introducing ethical analyses into the democratic policy-making process.

FOOD BIOTECHNOLOGY

'Biotechnology' has been defined as encompassing 'any technique that uses living organisms, to make or modify a product, to improve plants or animals, or to develop microorganisms for special uses'.[4] Clearly, in terms of food, such a definition includes many traditional practices in agriculture, food processing and food preservation – such as selective breeding of crops and animals, and the fermentation processes involved in the manufacture of bread, beer and dairy products. But the focus here is on the novel biotechnologies intro- duced in recent years, such as those based on genetic engineering (recombinant DNA technology), monoclonal antibodies and the new animal reproductive technologies (including *in vitro* fertilisation, embryo transfer and cloning). These are being increasingly employed in the food industry, often in powerful combinations. Subsequent use of the word 'biotechnology' in this chapter should be interpreted in terms of these modern applications.

Because of the very wide range of technologies, in the space available, the principal issues to be discussed will necessarily be addressed by reference to a few, quite specific, examples.

ETHICAL ISSUES IN FOOD BIOTECHNOLOGY

Ethical dilemmas arise when there appear to be good reasons for performing opposing actions. Reasons cited for employing new biotechnologies are generally couched in economic terms. Thus in the EU those sectors where biotechnology has a direct impact (e.g. pharmaceuticals, health-care and agriculture) account for 9% of the EU's gross added-value (about 450 billion European currency units) and about 8% of its employment (approximately nine million people). However, in terms of global competitiveness the EU lags behind the

USA and is also facing strong competition from Japan. The European Commission has expressed the view that

> by the year 2000 with an estimated world market of 100 billion ECU for the biotechnology industry, the Community growth rate will have to be substantially higher than at present to ensure that the Community will become a major producer of such products.[5]

The economic imperative is reflected in other official statements, which seek to sweep aside regulations thought to place the EU at a competitive disadvantage. For example, in the UK, a House of Lords Select Committee report argued that the only valid concerns about biotechnology relate to the nature of the product and not to the production process, so that 'There is no case for labelling a GMO (genetically modified organism) derived product differently from the same type of product not so derived'. Moreover, 'Work on further process based EC Directives should cease forthwith; and ... socio-economic need must not be introduced as an additional criterion in the product regulation of biotechnology'. The underlying assumption is that the products of biotechnology 'are likely to yield enormous future benefits to mankind' and that its appropriate employment can safely be left to the operations of the market, which should, itself, be freed of unnecessary regulation.[6]

But what regulations are necessary? Some of the characteristic features of the free market are that it responds:

- to wants rather than needs;
- to purchasing power rather than entitlement; and
- impulsively to transient influences (as is revealed frequently on the stock markets) rather than with circumspection.

In an extreme 'worst case' scenario, the world's wealth might be owned by one person who left everyone else to starve and destroyed the earth overnight for amusement. But less fantastic outcomes would also be a matter of serious concern, for example, if, as a result of widespread use of biotechnology, power were to be increasingly concentrated in the hands of directors of a few multi-national companies; if existing disparities of health and wealth were to be exacerbated; and if the sustainability of the biosphere were to be irremediably undermined. Regulations are therefore necessary, and because they concern (at least) humanity at large, any form of rational ethical assessment of biotechnology needs to examine the impacts of the features of the market identified above.

Food is a universal requirement, the production of which affects and is affected by the environment in which we all live. These stark facts imply that in addressing ethical aspects of food biotechnology it is the social dimension which is of paramount importance. Some may consider such questions are political rather than ethical, but 'Ethical issues transcend the different levels of human organization and, therefore, political systems embody ethical systems'.[7] My concerns here are thus with a branch of social ethics which is relevant to public policy, and which in turn will guide the implementation of necessary regulations on the employment of biotechnology in food production.

Social ethics might seem a somewhat novel concept, because ethics is popularly conceived of in terms of personal conduct. Even in other growing areas of applied ethics, such as medical ethics and business ethics, the dilemmas encountered are usually those facing individual practitioners in their professional roles. By contrast, what is at issue here is how, in democratic societies, we go about reaching policy decisions which both seek to benefit society as whole and also respect the (often divergent) interests of the various disparate groups within society.

Fundamental to such an objective is the notion of the 'social contract', 'an explicit or implied agreement ... that is taken to serve as the basis for social cooperation, governance and the rule of law'.[8] Ideally, such an agreement requires that all members of society have access to a scheme of ethical evaluation which is rational, unbiased, comprehensive and transparent. Unfortunately, these requirements are rarely met in practice. For example, the objectivity of the EC Group of Advisers on the Ethics of Biotechnology, which was set up in 1991, might be said to have been compromised by one of its three terms of reference: 'to advise the Commission in its legislative role as regards the ethical aspects of biotechnology with a view to improving public understanding and acceptance of it' (sic).[9] Moreover, the group of six Commission-appointed committee members holds meetings in private (although the number has now been increased to nine and some attempts are being made to seek the opinion of interest groups).

A PRINCIPLED APPROACH TO ETHICS

When the field of biomedical ethics was developing in the 1970s and early 1980s, there was considerable interest in the employment of frameworks of principles to facilitate the resolution of ethical dilemmas. A prominent approach was that advanced by Beauchamp and Childress,[10] who advocated a scheme which proposed that, in treating patients, health-care workers have prima facie obligations to show respect for four principles:

- autonomy (the decision-making capacities of autonomous persons)
- justice (fair distribution of benefits, risks and costs)
- nonmaleficence (avoidance of causation of harm)
- beneficence (provision of benefits and balancing them against risks and costs)

These four principles are 'drawn from the common morality ... the morality that all reasonable persons share and acknowledge ... common sense ethics as it is sometimes called'.[11]

In the last decade this 'principled' approach to ethics has been criticised as inadequate to the challenges of modern medicine, and alternative approaches, such as 'casuistry' and 'virtue theory', have been advocated. It is impossible to discuss the merits of such theories adequately here but, in any event, they would seem to be most clearly applicable, if at all, to ethical concerns at the personal level. Once we leave this level to deliberate on policy matters, such criticisms lose their edge. As noted by Beauchamp, 'When strangers meet in professional settings, character judgements (cf. virtue theory) will often play a less significant role than norms that express rights and appropriate procedures'. And, significantly: 'The same is true in the enforcement of institutional rules and in framing public policy'.[12]

The claim I wish to advance is that such principles, suitably translated within the context of food biotechnologies, provide a framework for ethical analysis which should facilitate appropriate public policy-making in democratic societies.

AN ETHICAL MATRIX

One important difference between the context for which the principled approach was originally devised and that to which it is here applied is the range of 'affected parties' or 'interest groups'. At its simplest, a decision in medicine might significantly affect only one person – the patient. In food production, typically, millions of people (including producers, processors, retailers and consumers), the physical and biological environments and, often, non-human animals, are liable to be affected, one way or another, by decisions on a new technology. For this reason, the principles need to be translated into terms which are meaningful to the different interest groups. Moreover, because the principles of 'respect for non-maleficence and beneficence' are reciprocally related, they are here combined as 'respect for well-being'. The, now, three principles (well-being, autonomy and justice), may be seen to correspond to three principal contemporary theories of ethics, namely, utilitarianism, deontological theory and Rawls' theory of 'justice viewed as fairness', respectively. Setting out these principles in a table, they form a matrix (see Table 1), which provides a framework for objective ethical analysis.[13]

	Well-being	**Autonomy**	**Justice**
Treated organism	e.g. Animal welfare	e.g. Behavioural freedom	Respect for *telos*
Producers (e.g. farmers)	Adequate income and working conditions	Freedom to adopt or not adopt	Fair treatment in trade and law
Consumers	Availability of safe food, acceptability	Respect for consumer choice (labelling)	Universal affordability of food
Biota	Conservation of the biota	Maintenance of biodiversity	Sustainability of biotic populations

Table 1 An Ethical Matrix showing, in twelve individual cells, the interpretation of respect for the three principles of well-being, autonomy and justice in terms appropriate to the interests of treated organisms (e.g. animals or crops), producers (e.g. farmers or biotechnology company employees) consumers and biota. For further details see the text.

(The designation of *biota*, defined as 'the animal and plant life of a region', as an interest group might seem unduly anthropomorphic. Yet concern seems justified both because wildlife populations, perhaps more commonly referred to collectively with reference to the *environment*, perform an essential role in maintaining ecological stability and because, for some people, all life forms possess intrinsic value which is worthy of moral respect: indeed, some environmental ethicists refer to the *biotic community*.)[14]

It is important to appreciate the aims and limitations of the Matrix:

- it seeks to provide a framework for rational analysis: the impacts defined for each of the 'cells' depend on rigorous examination of objective (often scientific) data

- the 'interest groups' can be defined to any desired degree of precision, e.g. within the category 'consumers' one might distinguish 'the elderly' or 'low-income families'
- construction of the Matrix is in principle ethically neutral: any *evaluation* process would require weighing or ranking of the different ethical impacts
- obligations to respect the different principles will not infrequently conflict, entailing a balance to be achieved either by one obligation overriding other/s or by the partial discharge of obligations
- whilst it might guide individual ethical judgements, the principal aim of the Matrix is to facilitate rational public policy decision-making by articulating the ethical dimensions of any issue in a way which is widely comprehensible.

We now need to consider ethical issues raised by employment of biotechnology in the food industry and to test the usefulness of the Matrix by applying it to specific examples. These examples are chosen from both the animal and plant fields to illustrate the different types of ethical impact which arise, and all involve transgenic techniques (genetic engineering).

BOVINE SOMATOTROPHIN USE IN DAIRYING

The most prominent example of a genetically engineered product used in animal agriculture is the hormone, bovine somatotrophin (also called somatotropin or growth hormone, and usually abbreviated to BST or BGH), which is manufactured by four multi-national companies. This pituitary gland hormone is now produced by recombinant-DNA techniques in a transgenic form of the common gut bacterium, *E. Coli*. Injected into cows, BST can substantially increase milk yields (galactopoiesis): increases of 15% are usually claimed, although in individual cases increases can vary from zero to over 50%. BST serves as a particularly valuable case study because, at the time of writing, it is licensed for use in the USA and several other countries but banned from commercial use in the EU, at least until the year 2000.

Ethical issues arise in several respects, namely, in terms of impacts on the treated animals, on milk producers (dairy farmers) and retailers, on consumers, on the environment and on the social and economic condition of whole societies, both nationally and globally.

In examining the ethical impacts of BST, or any new technology, it is important to realise that the existing situation is taken as a baseline. But that is itself problematical because current practice may fall far short of ethical acceptability; and it may be that the scrutiny to which we subject innovations will uncover previously unacknowledged defects. Moreover, the ethical acceptability of any technology is not solely to be measured by reference to current practices, however undesirable they might be, but also to other alternatives which we might introduce if we had a mind to. Subsequent comments are made with reference to Table 1.

Producers

There are, at least, two ways of interpreting this category, viz. producers of BST (the manufacturers) and milk producers (dairy farmers). The former seem certain to reap considerable financial benefits (cf. well-being), with global sales predicted to reach $1 billion per annum.

However, the benefits for dairy farmers will be highly variable. A US White House report issued in 1994 predicted that, at the assumed adoption rates, the returns per cow for the year 1999 will be +$3 for adopters and −$84 for non-adopters.[15] Such outcomes may be said to undermine producer autonomy, by forcing farmers to adopt BST, and to fail to respect fairness, by penalising farmers who are unprepared to profit from the discomfort, and in some cases suffering, of their animals (see below).

Dairy cows

Respect for well-being is compromised because BST use increases the incidence of several diseases. There has been much dispute between the manufacturing companies and their critics as to whether the increased morbidity is significant, in the sense that production-related disease is common in high-yielding cows because of the increased metabolic demands to which they are subjected. However, the fact remains that when the Monsanto BST product, Posilac, was licensed for use in the USA in February, 1994, the product label revealed that treated cows were at increased risk of 21 side-effects (many of which have painful symptoms), including:

increased cystic ovaries and disorders of the uterus; higher incidence of retained placenta; increased risk of clinical and

subclinical mastitis; increased digestive disorders such as indiges-
tion, bloat and diarrhoea; increased numbers of enlarged hocks
and lesions of the knee; disorders of the foot; and injection site
lesions which may remain permanent.[16]

Published data indicate that, even under the conditions of expert
management to be expected in research institute studies, substantial
increases in morbidity and mortality occurred following BST administration. For example, in one group of 62 cows treated with BST for
two years, eight cows died, whereas none of the 21 control cows
suffered a similar fate. In another study, 10% of cows had 'severe'
injection site swellings (>16cm long and >2cm high) and 50%
'moderate' swellings (10–16 cm long and 1–2 cm high) ten days after
BST administration, injections being given every fourteen days.[17] It is
unlikely that BST would prove commercially viable were such levels of
mortality and morbidity to be common in commercial practice.
Nevertheless, the fact they that have been recorded in experimental
studies suggests that cows treated with BST face significant risks.

What effect does BST use have on the principle of respect for
autonomy, translated for the animals as 'respect for behavioural
freedom' (see Table 1)? Clearly, the disease conditions cited above,
such as lameness, infringe behavioural freedom. But, even in the
absence of clinical disorders, freedom is constrained since fully
exploiting BST's galactopoietic effect demands use of concentrate
feeds. So-called zero-grazing (in which animals are kept permanently
indoors) might become the norm for many animals.

Translation of the principle of respect for justice as 'respect for
telos'[18] requires that consideration be given to the extent to which
BST use infringes the intrinsic nature of the animals. Some would
maintain that domesticated animals are already altered to serve
human ends and have acquired a new *telos*. However, all animals
(certainly higher mammals) can be said to have individual natures,
which would be severely altered by regular enforced disruptions of the
homeostatic processes controlling normal body function, such as are
induced by BST administration.

Consumers

With respect to well-being, two types of risks to human health
demand consideration – one resulting from milk avoidance, the other
from consumption of BST milk.

According to a consumer survey, were BST to be licensed in the EU, the number of consumers who would favour a total boycott of products associated with BST would reduce total milk consumption by 11%.[19] The public health implications of such a decrease become apparent when it is appreciated that milk is an important source of essential dietary components, such as calcium, proteins, vitamins and trace elements. For example, further reductions in calcium intake (of which 60% is derived from milk in the UK) are likely to exacerbate the increasing incidence of osteoporosis, which has reached almost epidemic proportions among postmenopausal women in the UK.

The other type of risk is that due to compositional changes in milk. The galactopoietic effect of BST is associated with an increase in the concentration in milk of insulin-like growth factor 1 (IGF1), a substance which is biologically active in humans. Concerns have been expressed that at the concentrations IGF1 attains in BST milk, and because it is protected from digestion by the milk protein, casein, it might have inappropriate effects on the cells of the consumer's intestinal tract.[20] The investigations performed (on rats) to test the safety of orally administered IGF1, on the basis of which BST was licensed for use in the USA, did not address the particular issue of IGF1's potential effects on gut cytokinetics, but regulatory authorities in both the USA and the EU continue to dismiss the hazard as insignificant.[21]

However, it is too restrictive an interpretation of well-being to limit discussion to threats to the physical health of consumers. There is much evidence that a majority oppose the introduction of BST. For example in two opinion surveys in the USA, 56% were 'very or somewhat concerned' and 69% 'strongly or somewhat opposed', respectively.[22] The unease experienced by such consumers would seem to represent a failure to respect the principle of well-being.

Respect for consumer autonomy, interpreted as freedom of choice, has also been infringed in the USA, where it has been illegal to label milk as 'non-BST', because it is claimed to be indistinguishable from BST milk. This offends two important aspects of autonomy, *voluntariness* and *disclosure of information*, which are not only ethical principles but also conditions essential to the efficient operation of a free market. The prevailing view of regulatory authorities and government advisers is that if the *product* resulting from use of biotechnology is essentially the same as that produced by traditional means consumers can have no interest in the matter. However, consumers may well wish to choose food produced by certain procedures and avoid that produced by others: after all, many choose to pay more for organic foods, which, as products, are often indistinguishable from non-organic foods. But there is a further flaw in the regulators' argument, because quite recently a means of distinguishing milk from cows treated with BST has been described, based on the slight difference in molecular structure between natural and manufactured forms of BST, which allows the latter's detection by immunological techniques.[23]

Respect for justice, interpreted as affordability, appears to be neither enhanced nor infringed: the introduction of BST has not led to a fall in the price of milk in the USA.

Biota

Manufacturers of BST claim that a strong argument in its favour is that the required amount of milk can be produced from fewer cows, thus reducing pollution. It is undoubtedly true that animal production has considerable adverse impacts on the environment. Thus, slurry, silage runoff and leached fertilisers contaminate soil and water, to the detriment of local biota, while methane gas (which cows emit in large amounts) is a greenhouse gas which contributes to global warming. A more efficient form of production, yielding the same amount of milk from fewer cows, might thus be said to respect *biotic conservation*, *biodiversity* and *sustainability*.

There are, however, a number of countervailing impacts of BST, which might offset the claimed benefits. First, BST use is likely to lead to a concentration of the dairy industry, with smaller numbers of large, highly intensive dairy farms. Since pollutants, such as manure and silage effluents, have serious effects on the local environment, intensification could well exacerbate existing problems. Second, since the galactopoietic effect of BST is dependent on high feed energy intake, adverse effects on the environment will be accentuated by increased dependence on fossil fuels, artificial fertilisers, farm and industrial machinery and transportation.

Summary

The comprehensive approach to ethical impacts provided by the framework of the Matrix reveals that there are several respects in which the prima facie ethical principles are undermined. Respect is shown for the well-being of manufacturers and some dairy farmers, and in certain ways the environment may benefit from reduced numbers of animals. But effects on animals, many dairy farmers, consumers and biota are generally negative. A full ethical analysis would, of course, need to address these issues from a global perspective. Suffice it to note that milk yields of most cattle in less developed countries are principally limited by feed supply, so that BST is unlikely to have beneficial effects and could induce heat stress in the animals. Serious economic consequences could also result if local markets in less developed countries were flooded with surplus dairy products from developed economies: after all, global competitiveness is the claimed *raison d'être* of technological innovation.

However, the Ethical Matrix does not aim to be prescriptive but only, by analysing the issues, to describe ethical impacts. The evaluation stage depends on the weighing of these impacts – and it is here that different outcomes will become apparent.

EC Group of Advisers Report

Thus, the EC Group of Advisors found BST to be 'ethically unobjectionable' and safe for both humans and animals, provided certain conditions are met, including:

- (4.1) cows do not suffer extreme pain or even discomfort that is disproportionate to the human good expected from use of the product
- (4.4) the level of somatic cells/ml of milk should not be higher than the concentration found in milk thus far produced by high [yielding] cows obtained through selective breeding
- (4.5) if it becomes possible to distinguish milk derived from BST-treated cows from other milk, then the vendors should be required to label it and its derivatives to allow free choice to buyers.

The report also declared that 'the question of marketing or non-marketing [of] BST in the European Community is mainly a political issue which should be discussed as such'.[24]

However, these recommendations raise many questions. How is the utilitarian calculus of paragraph 4.1 to be applied? Which particular level of somatic cells (indicative of subclinical mastitis) in selectively bred high-yielding cows is to be regarded as acceptable (cf. paragraph 4.4)? And does paragraph 4.5 imply that in the EU, contrary to the situation in the USA, labelling of milk is to be regarded as ethically obligatory, regardless of the costs of monitoring? Moreover, the suggestion that ethical and political issues should be discussed separately implies a belief in their independence from each other which is surprising, to say the least.

The analysis provided above, employing the Matrix (which for current purposes is summary in the extreme), provides a means of identifying the full range of issues of ethical significance and of readily determining the relative weight apportioned, by bodies such as the EC group of advisors, to the different ethical impacts.

THE FLAVR SAVR TOMATO

Another genetically engineered product which has achieved much prominence is the Flavr Savr tomato, produced by Calgene and retailed as a fresh fruit in the USA since 1994. Such fruit carry an antisense gene which reduces expression of polygalacturonase, a pectin-degrading enzyme, and hence delays excessive ripening and rotting. A number of advantages have been claimed. Growers can delay harvesting until the fruit is ripe, with less risk of damage to the fruit during this process; retailers deal with a product with longer shelf-life, which need not be refrigerated; and consumers can purchase a better-looking, longer-lasting tomato.

Since the general approach has already been outlined, the analysis in this case will be extremely brief and concentrate on its distinctive features. Doubtless, some tomato growers (cf. well-being) will benefit, while others will suffer loss of income. It is likely that major detrimental effects will be experienced in less developed countries, where the indigenous produce may lose out in international competition. In the USA, consumers have the choice of longer-lasting tomatoes, but a potential adverse feature is that the tomatoes carry a second transgene, which confers resistance to the antibiotic, kanamycin. This is a marker gene, which is a residuum of the production process. The UK Advisory Committee on Novel Foods and Processes has recently drawn attention to the inadvisability of increasing the numbers of antibiotic microorganisms in the environment,[25] but this is a likely outcome when seeds carrying the gene are excreted undigested, or when fruit are damaged or otherwise wasted.

On the positive side, consumer choice is respected in the USA by labelling, though affordability is challenged by the higher price of these tomatoes.

An issue which may strike some people as trivial is the question of respect for the *telos* of the tomato plant. Granted that tomatoes are unable to perceive the presence within themselves of foreign genes, a view is advanced that the intrinsic nature, not only of sentient beings but also of plants, deserves human respect. The attitude is grounded in a metaphysical view of the nature of existence which is held by those who have been characterised as 'participators' in the world, rather than 'dominators' or 'stewards'.[26]

Transgenic tomatoes pose a different set of ethical problems from those discussed for BST, and negative impacts seem fewer.

TRANSGENIC ANIMALS

The development of transgenic animals for food production lags behind that involving microbes (such as BST) and plants (such as transgenic tomatoes). The insertion of extra and/or foreign genes into the pronucleus of the single cell embryo has been used in several research programmes aimed at increasing the growth rates of farm animals. In perhaps the most notorious example of this approach, pigs bearing genes for human growth hormone (Beltsville pigs, named after the institute in the USA where the research was conducted) were induced to grow faster and leaner than normal pigs. However, the animals suffered from several extremely unpleasant pathological conditions. In the words of a pioneer of this type of research:

> Essentially all transgenic GH [i.e. with additional Growth Hormone genes] pigs and sheep have had serious physiological as well as anatomical problems ... including altered endocrine profiles and metabolism, insufficient thermoregulatory capacity, joint pathology (lameness and arthritis), low libido, infertility and an increased susceptibility to pneumonia.[27]

Not all transgenic animals suffer a similar fate, and the sheep referred to in the quotation with which this chapter begins appear to live essentially normal lives, except that their high commercial value might lead to some restrictions on their freedom of behaviour. Such sheep are examples of animals termed bioreactors, which secrete valuable pharmaceuticals in their milk. However, the procedures by which the transgene is introduced into the single cell embryo are highly inefficient so that large numbers of embryos either fail to develop into adult sheep or do so, but fail to secrete the desired pharmaceutical in their milk: less than 5% of micro-injected embryos become transgenic sheep. It is for this reason that a request was made for permission to sell the surplus animals for meat. This specific request led to the setting up of a committee to 'consider the moral and ethical concerns ... that may arise from the use of food products derived from food production programmes involving such organisms'. The committee saw no overriding ethical objections which would require absolute prohibition of use of animals containing copy genes of human origin as food, but it recommended discouragement of the use of ethically sensitive genes (originating from humans and certain non-human animals) and labelling to protect religious and cultural sensibilities (for example, to indicate where plant foods contained genes of animal origin).[28]

Again, however, the principal focus of ethical concern was taken to be the nature of the food product, the report claiming that 'wider ethical issues' were not within the committee's remit. However, it can be argued that the process by which transgenic animals are produced is important in any meaningful ethical evaluation. Indeed, the fact that the report cited as relevant the notion of 'moral taint' (exemplified by the unacceptability of using for transplant purposes the organs of a prisoner who had died under torture), would seem to acknowledge the validity of this viewpoint.

To what extent, then, is it reasonable to claim that animal transgenesis confers 'moral taint' on resulting food products? Glossy photographs in publicity brochures of sheep roaming freely on sunlit hillsides might persuade the uninitiated that such an assertion is misguided in the extreme. Yet, the reality is otherwise. The micro-injection process by which transgenic farm animals are produced leads to random incorporation of the transgene, with unpredictable, and often inappropriate, side-effects due to insertion site and mutational effects. These often result in early embryo mortality, but some embryos may survive to term and be born with various defects. Other techniques involved also have adverse effects on animal welfare, such as *in vitro* embryo culture, which often results in oversize fetuses that need to be delivered by Caesarian section, and embryo transfer, which also often involves surgical procedures.[29] It is hardly irrational to wish to have a choice as to whether to support, through one's purchasing power, programmes of this type.

With reference to the Matrix, many significant issues parallel those identified in the discussion of BST, namely, those concerning animal well-being, behavioural freedom and *telos*; and consumer freedom of choice. In 1993, public concern over such matters led the UK Ministry of Agriculture to set up a second ethical committee, this time to consider the ethical implications of emerging technologies in animal breeding. Among the conclusions of its report were the following three principles relating to animal welfare:

- harms of a certain degree and kind ought under no circumstances to be inflicted on an animal
- any harm to an animal, even if not absolutely impermissible, nonetheless requires justification and must be outweighed by the good which is realistically sought in so treating it
- any harm which is justified by the second principle ought, however, to be minimised as far as is reasonably possible.[30]

By contrast with the opinion of the EC Group of Advisers on BST, discussed above, the first of these principles recognises that a utilitarian (cost/benefit) approach is inadequate to a sound ethical evaluation of new biotechnologies. The committee's report makes a useful contribution to public awareness and debate on food biotechnology and wisely warns that a public suspicion of farming may arise:

> unless those who are engaged in the development and application of these technologies endeavour to be sensitive to public concerns, open to debate with interested parties and supportive of a reasonable system of regulation, provision of information and labelling.

CONCLUSIONS

The new biotechnologies applied to food raise important ethical questions, the democratic responses to which need to be reflected in public policy. Current arrangements for addressing these issues tend to undermine public participation by dividing them into scientific, economic and 'ethical' questions (the latter frequently interpreted, narrowly, to refer to intuitive abreactions), which can then be 'dealt with' by appropriate experts. There is little appreciation of Winner's insight on the profound difference between the notion that 'technology requires legislation' and the notion that 'technology is legislation'.[31]

If the general public is to be involved in decisions on what should be permitted, regulated (and how) or proscribed, procedures need to be introduced to facilitate public participation in the debate. Consensus conferences such as that held in 1994 in the UK on the subject of plant biotechnology, which involve the committed participation over a period of several weeks of a small, cross-sectional group of lay persons, represent a bold approach to public education and involvement in policy-making.[32] But it is doubtful whether their extension is a realistic means of increasing public participation, not least because they are expensive to run.

The Ethical Matrix described in this chapter is proposed as a framework for encouraging wider public participation in policy-making. Based on 'the common morality', it aims to provide a comprehensive overview of ethically relevant issues and to facilitate transparency in decision-making by advisory and regulatory bodies. Few matters are of such immediate concern to us as the food we eat, and for that reason alone the effectiveness of the Matrix in promoting informed and rational ethical deliberation might well be tested on the rising tide of novel food biotechnologies. While there would be dangers in presenting the Matrix, simplistically, as a device for arriving at ethical judgements, there are a number of settings in which it might be employed appropriately and effectively to promote rational discussion, for example in the classroom, seminar room and roundtable workshop, as well as in educational texts, professional magazines and consumer group publications.

NOTES

1   MAFF, *Report of the Committee on the Ethics of Genetic Modification and Food Use* (London, HMSO, 1993) p.1.
2   Commission of the European Community (1993) *Biotechnology and genetic engineering: what Europeans think about it in 1993*, p.48.
3   Glover, J., *Causing Death and Saving Lives* (Harmondsworth, Penguin, 1977).
4   Persley, G.L. *Beyond Mendel's Garden: biotechnology in the service of world agriculture* (Wallingford, CAB International, 1990) p.1.
5   European Commission (1993) White Paper on *Growth, competitiveness and employment*, p.116.
6   House of Lords Select Committee on Science and Technology (1993) *Regulation of the UK biotechnology industry and global competitiveness* (HL paper 80) pp.62–63.
7   Zimmerman, A.D. (1995) 'Towards a more democratic ethic of technological governance', *Science, Technology and Human Values* 20, 86–107.
8   Thompson, P.B., Matthews, R.J. and van Ravenswaay, E.O., *Ethics, Public Policy and Agriculture* (New York, Macmillan, 1994) p.8. Any number of sources could be cited here, but this is a very useful introduction to the whole field of agricultural ethics.
9   European Commission, Secretariat General (undated) *Activities of the European Commission in the field of bioethics*, p.1.
10 Beauchamp, T.L. and Childress, J.F. *Principles of Biomedical Ethics*, 4th edn (New York and Oxford, Oxford University Press, 1994).

118   Ben Mepham

11 Beauchamp, T.L. (1994) 'Principles and other emerging paradigms in bioethics', *Indiana Law Journal* 69, 957.
12 Ibid., p.969.
13 For further details on the Ethical Matrix, see, for example, Mepham, T.B., 'Ethical impacts of biotechnology in dairying', in *Progress in Dairy Science*, Phillips, C.J.C. (ed.) (Wallingford, CAB International, 1996) pp. 375–395; Mepham, T.B. (1995) 'An ethical matrix for animal production', *New Farmer and Grower* 46, 14–16; Mepham, T.B. and Forbes, J.M. (1995) 'Ethical aspects of the use of immunomodulation in farm animals', *Livestock Production Science* 42, 265–272; Mepham, T.B. (1996) 'A framework for the ethical auditing of animal biotechnologies', *Animal Breeding* (in press).
14 Rolston III, H., 'Environmental ethics: values and duties to the natural world', in *Applied Ethics*, Winkler E.R. and Coombes, J.R. (eds) (Oxford and New York, Blackwell, 1991) pp. 271–292.
15 Office of Management and Budget, the Executive Branch of the Federal Government (the White House) (January 1994) *Use of bovine somatotropin in the United States: its potential effect*, p.30.
16 Monsanto Company (1993) Posilac package insert.
17 Cole, W.J. *et al.* (1992) 'Response of dairy cows to high doses of sustained release bovine somatotropin administered during two lactations. 2. Health and reproduction', *Journal of Dairy Science* 75, 111–123; Pell, A.N. *et al.* (1992) 'Effects of prolonged-release formulation of sometribove (n-methionyl bovine somatotropin) on Jersey cows', *Journal of Dairy Science* 75, 3416–3431.
18 See Holland, A., 'Artificial lives: philosophical dimensions of farm animal biotechnology', in *Issues in Agricultural Bioethics*, Mepham, T.B., Tucker, G.A. and Wiseman, J. (eds) (Nottingham, Nottingham University Press, 1995) pp. 293–305.
19 Commission of the European Community (1993) *Concerning bovine somatotrophin (B.S.T.)* COM (93) 331 final.
20 Mepham, T.B., Schofield, P.N., Zumkeller, W. and Cotterill, A.M. (1994) 'Safety of milk from cows treated with bovine somatotrophin', *Lancet* 344, 1445–1446; Xian, C.J., Shoubridge, C.A. and Read, L.C. (1995) 'Degradation of insulin-like growth factor-1 in the adult rat gastrointestinal tract is limited by a specific antiserum or the dietary protein casein', *Journal of Endocrinology* 146, 215–225.
21 Juskevich, J.C. and Guyer, C.G. (1990) 'Bovine growth hormone: food safety evaluation', *Science* 249, 875–884; MAFF (1994) Paper prepared by officials of the Department of Health and the Veterinary Medicines Directorate for the Consumer Panel meeting 27.4.94. Reference: CP(94)18/5–6.
22 Smith, B.J. and Warland, R.H., 'Consumer responses to milk from BST supplemented cows', in *Bovine Somatotropin and Emerging Issues*, Hallberg, M.C. (ed.) (Boulder, Colorado, Westview Press, 1992) pp. 243–264.
23 Erhard, E.H., Kellner, J., Schmidhuber, J., Schams, D. and Losch, U. (1994) 'Identification of antigenic differences of recombinant and pituitary bovine growth hormone using monoclonal antibodies', *Journal of Immunoassay* 15, 1–19.

24 European Commission Group of Advisers on the Ethical Aspects of Biotechnology (1993) *The ethical implications of the use of performance-enhancers in agriculture and fisheries* (Rapporteurs M. Warnock and M. Siniscalo).

25 Advisory Committee on Novel Foods and Processes (1994) *Report on the use of antibiotic resistance markers in genetically modified food organisms* London, MAFF.

26 Kockelkoren, P.J.H. (1993) *Ethical Issues in Plant Biotechnology* (Ministry of Agriculture, Nature Management and Fisheries, The Netherlands).

27 Pinkert, C.H., Dyer, T.J., Kooyman, D.L. and Kiehm, D.J. (1990) *Domestic Animal Endocrinology* 7, 1–18.

28 MAFF 1993, op. cit.

29 Moore, C.J. and Mepham, T.B. (1995) 'Transgenesis and animal welfare', *Alternatives to Laboratory Animals* 23, 380–397.

30 MAFF, *Report of the Committee to consider the Ethical Implications of Emerging Technologies in Animal Breeding* (London, HMSO, 1995).

31 Winner, L., *Autonomous Technology: technics-out-of-control as a theme in political thought* (Cambridge, MIT Press, 1977) p.323.

32 *Report of the UK National Consensus Conference on Plant Biotechnology* (London, Science Museum, 1994).

Chapter 8

Bread to biotechnology: cultural aspects of food ethics

Leslie Gofton

INTRODUCTION

Food is such a fundamental part of human existence that it would perhaps be inconceivable for it not to be bound up with ethics. Moreover, like ethical beliefs, food choices are not simply a set of decisions that individuals make, but 'a thinking framework' which pre-forms the way in which we see the world.

Food ethics – comprising those aspects of food which bear on moral principles, which relate to human character and are involved in moral duty and obligation to the community – is certainly a current concern. For example, is it morally acceptable to mistreat, or even use animals at all, in the process of food production? Is it acceptable for a small, privileged group to have the lion's share of the world's resources, including food, while the rest do not have enough? Is it ethical for producers to market foods which damage health? The issues multiply out of control, as though the food producer, lauded until recently for the conquest of shortages, had become the sorcerer's apprentice, unleashing a flood of anxieties and misgivings about how it has been accomplished, and what the consequences might be. This is Ulrich Beck's[1] *Risikogessellschaft* (Risk Society), where confidence in technological and scientific 'progress' has turned out to be a chimera, involving risks which no one can foresee. The 'logic' of the food scientist and technologist, allied with market economics, has produced battery farming, bovine somatotrophin (BST), bovine spongiform encephalopathy (BSE) and biotechnology.

Yet surely this is only part of the story. Food production in recent times has also involved the conquest of diseases of plants and animals, and a technological revolution multiplying food production many times over. A key question, then, concerns the perception of this history: why is food seen as the arena for ethical conflicts, for problems and risks, in the midst of unparalleled food quality and surfeit? The answer lies in the culture within which food uses occur.

CULTURAL ASPECTS OF FOOD

Culture is what marks humankind off from the animal kingdom, and also divides person from person. The term refers to all material, symbolic and intellectual products of human societies, everything from religion, science, art and philosophy, down to flint arrowheads and chewing gum wrappers. Cultures have always made the closest possible connection between ethics and food. 'Commensality', sharing food, is the most fundamental expression of human friendship and sociability. The word for bread is included in the English *com-pan-ion* and the French *co-pain*, or friend. Neolithic remains show that from earliest times human groups have been formed around the processes of acquiring and distributing food: anthropologists still find that rules concerning the gathering of food crops or the division of the carcass are among the most important ethical imperatives. According to Robertson Smith: 'Those who eat and drink together are by this very act tied to one another by a bond of friendship and mutual obligation'.[2] Van Gennep[3] believes that the rite of eating together is a 'rite of incorporation, of physical union'. The sharing of meals is reciprocal, he argues, and hence the exchange of food constitutes the confirmation of a bond.

This has endured, even as societies have changed. Ewart Evans[4] describes village life around 1900, with yeast passed from house to house in 'bread circles', and then passed round again to brew beer. Beer itself became the medium for the expression of social solidarity in the public houses of the industrial age, involving rituals of exchange and a subculture which excluded all but the 'insiders' of the correct age, gender and locality.[5]

It is on these interdependencies, rights and obligations that the survival of a society may depend. Amartya Sen[6] showed that famines are the consequence not of a failure of food production, but of changes in the system of food entitlement. When the system by which food is distributed and allocated within a particular society breaks down, large numbers of people can find themselves without the social entitlements to food, and may starve. Food, then, not only symbolises cultural values, but also forms a medium through which social relationships are expressed, from the intimate, face-to-face relations within the family, to the relations between regions and nations. Gellner[7] suggests that as the relative importance of these relationships changes, perception of risk increases, as global forces replace small-group, neighbourhood 'local' relationships with formalised national and international relationships. Essentially, 'face-to-face' contact has been replaced by distant, abstract legalities; risk increases as intimacy loses its importance.

FOOD AND MORAL CATEGORIES

Perceptions of food vary across and within cultures. What is found delicious or disgusting may change radically from one valley to the next, and insults based on the diet of neighbouring groups – 'frog', 'kraut', 'haggis', etc. – are found throughout the world. Disgust over the food habits of other groups seems to function as the most basic of social barriers, marking insiders from outsiders, and translating cultural differences into feelings of repugnance and distance.

But how does it work? Mary Douglas[8] looked at the rules of the Jewish food system, and asked the question – why should Hebrews be forbidden to eat pork or other mysterious objects of taboo, such as the hyrax? Some argue that this is a kind of 'folk wisdom', which relates to real dangers. Thus, trichinosis can result from eating pig meat which has gone off, a big risk in a desert environment. Douglas argues, however, that the prohibition is not medical, but, like other rules about disgust, related to the way in which the group lived, and marked itself off from others. Nomadic sheep and goat herders in the Middle East feel themselves distinct from settled agriculturalists and urban dwellers and the animals they keep show that distinctness. Pigs cannot be herded over long distances; *ergo*, pig-keeping in itself can differentiate agri-cultures from nomad cultures. Structuralists argue that this becomes part of a system of general rules which relate not just to taboos, disgust and food, but to all kinds of judgements and cognitions of the world. Classifying certain animals as 'non-food' parallels or mimics rules concerning, say, appropriate sexual partners, or principles of right and wrong under the law.

Douglas argues that this is a universal phenomenon; that food rules relating to acceptability and disgust are essentially aesthetic, rather than physiologically based, and that they are expressions of fundamental principles underpinning the culture of groups who formulate and follow these rules. Food values can be used to communicate all manner of social meanings and values. The Kwakiutl, in British Columbia, display and claim status at feasts (potlatches) by 'fighting with property'.[9] Foods mark boundaries between age groups, castes, or men and women. Everywhere, food is used to sacralise, as a symbol of spiritual powers, as a medium for communion with the divine, in rituals such as *carne-val*, dedicated to meat, or marking seasons with fasting, abstinence and then feast.

Sidney Mintz[10] sees our sense of time, and our reaction to and understanding of the world, coming from seasonal food availability. New food production systems, which make virtually any foods available all the year round, and the engineering of tastes to incorporate sweetness, or 'mouth feel', result, he argues, in generalised cultural changes, as the meaning of time cycles, seasonal feasts and religious festivals, and the connections between them, are undermined. This clearly has implications for how these relate to our ethical frameworks, and food is deeply intertwined in the development of these systems.

THE EUROPEAN TRADITION

In classical Greece, sacrifice brought food to the heart of the spiritual and social order. The sacrificed animal was burnt in order to unite sacred and profane. The Gods partook of the smoke from the sacrificial pyre, while the 'remains', the flesh, were divided between members of the community, the polis, following strict, precise principles of butchery – subsequently the basis of mathematics and the physical sciences.[11]

This emphasis on the connection between the social order and eating developed, by the Middle Ages, into the conventions of the feast.[12] Foods have now acquired a particular relation to social status. Certain kinds of food are reserved for the highest ranks, and the different estates, age groups and gender groups are expected to adhere to strict rules which regulate the consumption process according to moral principles. Various rules of abstinence are enforced periodically for all lay people, and perennially for some members of the church. The connection of food with piety is almost universal, although the practices involved vary widely. Many social and religious rituals employ eating, or not eating, particular foods to express beliefs, or to symbolise group membership.

Stephen Mennell,[13] following Elias,[14] sees modern food habits and appetites developing from broader social changes. Elias related changes in personality and forms of cultural expression from the

Middle Ages to early modern times to very broad social changes, particularly the problems of control related to state formation. Broad social changes, in this view, relate to micro changes in the psychology and personality of the individual, and the expression of emotion, manners, taste and lifestyle.

Taste and appetite, Mennell avers, like personality, arise as a result of the transition from the medieval oscillation between plenty and want to a situation where discrimination at table, with food supplies stabilised and secure, is more important. He sees this as an aspect of the broader shift with which Elias is mainly concerned, between external, material constraints – such as supplies of food, and rules regulating their usage and disposal – and self-constraints, such as internalised models of behaviour and standards of aspiration and conduct.

Food consumption comes to embody ever more rigid internalised systems of control. As food availability ceases to be a problem, eating becomes an expression of self-control (quite literally) with a premium placed on a slim body and obesity being abjured. In pathological cases, these psychological tendencies can lead to heavily distorted patterns of 'over control', as in bulimia and anorexia.

The history of food habits, then, enables us to understand the ways in which taken-for-granted habits and beliefs have evolved. As Elias argues, even a simple behaviour such as handling a fork cannot be understood without relating it to a long, complex process of historical development, and to a nexus of other social institutions. What we take to be natural and universal turns out to be cultural, and highly specific to particular places and times.[15] It is the connection to other social institutions which needs to be addressed.

FISH AND CHIPS, EUGENICS AND THE NATURAL DOMESTICITY OF THE FEMALE

'Supermarket culture' has produced, it is said, an ill-fed and ill-disciplined generation that expects gratification immediately, and have scant respect for others. Junk food, snacking and 'grazing' or 'eating on the hoof', are replacing the family meal, and thereby accelerating the breakdown of 'family values'. According to 'This England' in 1986: 'Nowadays, children mostly arrive home from school to an empty house ... The television is provided to keep (the child) quiet until (mother) arrives home from work in an office or shop. Poor mum is too tired then to listen to childish chatter. She has no time to bake a cake or prepare a nourishing meal of stew and dumplings, so she feeds her family on deep frozen microwaved convenience foods ... Soaring crime rates and a breakdown of morals are the ultimate effects of evil. But the cause lies in the home ... Whatever changes the family unit will eventually destroy the nation'.[16]

Yet this is misleading. Social historians[17] have pointed out that this dual concern about children and adolescents being 'out of control', and the decline of 'traditional food habits' linking to the breakdown of the family, was just as apparent at the beginning of the industrial society as it is at the end. Study of time budget data[18] reveals that housewives in the early 1980s actually spent more time with their children than those in 1950, when the 'housewife' role was still very much the norm.

But we are certainly consuming more 'fast foods'. In the UK, the National Food Survey[19] shows that British consumers are buying more ready-made meals than ever. Total sales rose by 10% during the thirteen years from 1980–93, and by 1993 accounted for 35% of total food purchases. Convenience foods now provide 29% of our total energy.[20] Americans, according to Sennauer, Asp and Kinsey,[21] feel 'dollar rich and time poor'. Real incomes are rising, but as demands on (finite) time increase it becomes relatively more scarce and hence of greater value. This is strongly related to changes in women's roles: the US labour force participation rate for women now is well over 50% and over 70% for married women 35–41 years old. These women not only work in the labour force but continue to do most of the work inside the home, including cooking and food shopping. Changed attitudes to, and usage of, convenience products is a direct consequence of this: the majority of households in the UK and the USA now own microwave cookers.

This is not an uncontroversial conclusion, however. Schwartz Cowan[22] points out that in the early stages of industrialisation, there was a prevalent belief that new labour-saving domestic technologies such as piped water, iron stoves and packaged foods were producing 'leisured' housewives with little to do. She argues that, on the contrary, these 'labour-saving' devices simply resulted in a transfer of work from men to women, and that women did more work as a consequence, freeing masculine time for work in factories and offices. Nevertheless, prevailing beliefs insisted on the naturalness of this division of labour between men and women, and that, for the sake of society, a woman's place had to be in the home.

This message was reinforced in the schools. In the UK, the teaching of 'domestic science' to girls was believed to be essential to the health of the nation. Walton[23] tied these ideas about the importance of women's role to the eugenics movement, influential around the turn of the century, which argued that the future of the nation could only be based on 'selective breeding' to improve the 'gene pool'. In his study of the rise of fish and chips as a fast food at the end of the nineteenth century, Walton showed that there was great concern over the socially corrosive effects of the new shops, which were believed to be dens of iniquity, leading young people, especially girls, into immoral behaviour. The dish itself was held to be nutritionally inferior but more important, an abnegation of the moral responsibilities of the housewife.

This attitude, unfavourably contrasting convenience food with 'real' food, remains rooted in national consciousness. Recent changes seem to arise from the emancipation of women, but the old 'traditions' remain strong. In her South Wales study, Anne Murcott[24] found that although many of the abused wives of unemployed men were themselves working, they nevertheless remained responsible for putting a 'proper, cooked meal' on the table – which was often, in fact, the flashpoint for domestic violence. Other work has shown that, although most women are now doing paid jobs, they retain their old domestic responsibilities too, aided by new technologies such as microwave ovens and 'fast' foods, 'junk' foods, 'convenience' foods and ready meals.

Nicky Charles[25] argues that the rise in working opportunities and the 'liberation' of women can be seen rather as the outcome of broader economic forces. Women have been drawn into the workplace as production processes have become more automated and computerised. While workforces are also being reduced and casualised, operatives in factories are becoming de-skilled and labour organisations disempowered. According to this view, women workers suit enterprises requiring 'flexible', low-cost, part-time labour which can be taken on or laid off easily. Consequently, the demise of the 'traditional' household, and the rise of convenience eating, derive from an economic system which seeks to exploit women, rather than the 'self-interest' of women reneging on their 'natural' duties.

In any case, our notion of the 'traditional housewife' role may well rest on shaky foundations. Pahl[26] argues that what we see as a logical and 'natural' division of labour between men and women represents only a partial and temporary departure from what were much more diverse and integrated role relations before industrialism. He also argues that the post-industrial lifestyles of groups most strongly affected by the disappearance of stable, long-term male employment in single occupations have returned to a more integrated pattern of household provisioning, and social roles in which male and female take part in providing a range of household services.[27]

Relations between work, employment, kin and household arrangements are complex, and arrangements are dynamic as situations change and develop.

> Children, elderly parents, new partners, siblings and au pairs come and go. More serial monogamy, more stepchildren, more 'care in the community', all have to be meshed with just-in-time production systems, flexitime, job sharing, round the clock provision of services and greater demands for travel and mobility consequent upon enlarged markets and more personal negotiation based on increased flexibility.[28]

Gershuny's work also shows that it is wrong to assume a connection between changes in the kinds of products consumed (more convenience foods) and the behaviour of people (more working women). Increases in consumption of products or categories of food may be the consequence of population shifts – for example, increased numbers of single people without the resources or social needs to prepare food in 'traditional' ways – or alternative behaviours, such as changes in priorities. Most research shows that modern families place much greater emphasis on other kinds of domestic activities, and the home itself is now used for a whole range of leisure, social and educational pursuits, which change the significance of cooking and food. Pasi Falk[29] argues that the modern meal places much more emphasis, in any case, on the exchange of words, and on the social interactions involved. The nutritional and social importance of food *per se* is declining, and food consuming is becoming a 'side involvement'.[30]

Concern about food habits, then, often reflects anxieties about changes in the status of men, and in the traditional conception of the masculine role, which rested on domesticated and subordinated women. Rather than simply being a consequence of changed behaviour and social roles, new food habits are also a result of economic pressures on the household, due to technological changes in the nature of work (computerisation, de-skilling, casualised and feminised workforces) which themselves derive from changes in the nature of markets and systems of production. Unstable, highly competitive and saturated markets for goods and services, now established in global markets, have generated the need for workforces which can be used, in the French expression, as *amortisseurs*, shock absorbers, to be used and dispensed with as the market dictates.

This creates pressure on households in the way they use their resources, and destabilises many of their institutions, such as food habits and meal structures. Essentially, meal patterns which assumed a symbolic and ritual significance as expressions of social status, roles and relations, as well as fitting a particular division of labour, are now increasingly inappropriate for the new roles, responsibilities and priorities of members of the post-industrial household. New ethical significance attaches to food as these priorities change, and as resources within the household are redeployed in order to cope.

FOOD RISKS AND TRANS-SCIENCE

Food in the future faces an enormous paradox. Food production and marketing have resulted in high-quality food being produced in large quantities for developed countries. Yet concerns about food are growing, and there are significant ethical problems related to what kinds of food are produced, the methods of production and their side-effects, who consumes it, what effects it has on consumers, and what the consequences of this will be for the world as a whole.

Why should this be? After centuries seeking to solve the problem of food shortage, and using different kinds of food to symbolise prestige and status, why has food now become the focal point for concerns about the ethics of social order and its relation to the natural order?

The increasing concern about food is certainly attributable in part to the influence of mass media, which can 'amplify' public concern over this and many other social issues. But it is also attributable to the nature of eating itself.[31] Alan Beardsworth[32] argues that the ambivalence of eating is the most important factor. Food sustains life and health, and promotes pleasure and satisfaction but may also be the basis for illness and disease, and produce vomiting and nausea. Also, we may be 'polluted' by food if it contains inappropriate or disgusting elements, or has been prepared improperly. This constant tension between the needs it fulfils and the dangers it threatens creates inevitable anxieties.

Culture solves this problem, suppressing and controlling these anxieties by way of customs and traditions which prescribe and proscribe on the manner and form of food intake. Food habits become traditions imbuing the process with a taken-for-granted probity which permits the individual to proceed without questioning the issues raised by this ambivalence.

The authority of these traditional guidelines on selection and avoidance is now challenged. Competing food 'facts' now come from a range of sources, about the items we choose, the mode of preparation, hygiene and ethical acceptability. Although, in some cases, family influence remains strong, making sense of these facts devolves more and more to the individual, now without the guidance of conventions and social norms.

As individuals make these judgements, science seems unable to provide answers to their questions. Many cannot be answered scientifically. Although formulated in scientific terms, and requiring an answer in terms of fact, these are 'trans-scientific' questions, transcending science's ability to produce clear and unequivocal answers. For instance, because of the extreme variability in nutritional requirements from one person to another, it is extremely difficult to come up with overall nutritional standards. So science cannot offer a simple answer to 'What should we eat?'

Science has acquired enormous prestige by answering such questions yet, increasingly, scientific formulation of a theory or a problem (for example, the greenhouse effect) leads to the public asking questions to which a straightforward answer cannot be offered (for example, is the world getting hotter?). Anxiety over food, then, derives from a decline in the authority of tradition and the inability of science to provide an alternative. At the same time, our disillusion with the modern world and its way with animals and nature has taken the form of a reaction against the ways in which food is produced and farmed animals are treated.

HEALTH, ECOLOGY AND ANIMAL WELFARE

Compassion in World Farming, reporting on the poultry industry,[33] claimed that out of the 670 million chickens killed every year, 180 million suffered from malformed and crippled legs as a consequence of selective breeding. These, it was asserted, suffer more than any other livestock, including veal calves, in the production process. Every day, Americans kill 25 million chickens, while Europeans consume 340 million eggs. Eighty-five per cent of all hens live their lives in batteries.

Concern about and reaction to the treatment of animals has grown rapidly over the past few years. Between 1984 and 1994, the number of Britons claiming to be vegetarian doubled, from 2% to 4.5%. Some estimates put the proportion of the population 'avoiding meat' as 12%, with women being twice as likely as men to do so. One in eight young women avoid meat, which makes them the most likely of all sections of the population to do so. Food activists see the sheer scale of animal production as one of the most daunting aspects of the problem. Opponents regard these systems as fundamentally inhumane, at the very least, while proponents of 'animal rights' seek to get the law changed.

Yet the idea that animals can have rights is debatable. Some object that to see animals as having rights involves a category mistake, since rights can only, sensibly, be ascribed to humans. Animals lie outside the arena of ethical choice. This position leads to regarding animals as no different from inanimate objects, and, as Descartes believed, incapable of suffering in the way that humans can. Others argue that this view neglects the essential foundations of ethical thought, which involve the process of weighing others' interests against one's own. Without the sympathy and imagination required, ethical thought makes no sense. The judgement seems to lie along a continuum leading, at one extreme, to 'big brown eyes' anthropomorphism, and at the other to an almost psychopathic refusal to empathise with another creature, however similar to our own might be the nature and quality of its consciousness and experience of the world.

Keith Thomas[34] has argued that our attitudes to animals and the countryside have changed as we have come to depend less upon the natural world in the process of wealth creation. When we worked and lived close to other creatures in our day to day lives, the boundary between humanity and nature was more of a direct issue, and a 'man-centred' view of the universe, in which all creatures were there to serve man's purposes, was the natural defence. Ethical considerations were not extended to animals, birds, or the landscape, since they were considered subordinate to human purposes, and not part of the 'moral universe'.

As urbanisation progressed, and we grew more remote from animals and nature in terms of day to day contact, they became symbols of the world pure and uncorrupted. Man is part of the natural order, rather than at its centre, and begins to see other creatures and nature as, in a sense, sharing a fellowship. More and more animals are taken into companionship with humans, and given honorary human status. Small wonder that it becomes increasingly difficult for large sections of the population to treat creatures in whom such important values and symbolic meanings are invested simply as food. At the same time, many aspects of our modern world are becoming 'technicised',[35] and in that sense, dehumanised. Raphael Samuel[36] argues that the movements protesting against the cruelty of the trade in calves, and animal rights in general, are a consequence of the failure of mainstream politics to engage mass support on moral issues. In yet another paradox, as we begin to see animals and nature as deserving of the same treatment as human beings, we are also beginning to treat human beings, and natural things, more like machines.

THE 'MCDONALDIZATION' OF SOCIETY

Although the rise of the 'fast food' industry has often been criticised for the loss of quality and individuality which it represents, George Ritzer[37] argues that, in one sense, it poses a wider threat to the way in which we live. McDonald's, the fast food chain, has become a sacred icon of America. However, 'McDonaldization', 'the process by which the principles of the fast food restaurant are coming to dominate more and more sectors of American society as well as the rest of the world', applies not only to restaurants, but also to education, work, travel, leisure, dieting, politics and the family.

The McDonald brothers based their business on the quantifiable principles of speed, volume and low price. Customers were offered a highly circumscribed menu using assembly line procedures for cooking and serving food. In place of trained cooks, the limited menu allowed them to break down food preparation into simple, repetitive tasks that could be learned quickly even by those stepping into a commercial kitchen for the first time. They pioneered the use of specialised restaurant workers such as 'grill men', 'shake men', 'fry men', and 'dressers' (those who put the extras on burgers and who wrap them). They developed rules and regulations dictating what workers should do, and even what they should say.

'McDonaldization' is the outcome of a series of rationalisation processes that had been occurring throughout the twentieth century. One main feature of this is efficiency. Processes, goods and services that can be easily quantified tend to be suited to this way of thinking. The underlying assumption is that something which offers demonstrably more for our money, or simply more, must be better. Also, time saving is an important element. Customers are encouraged to compare the time spent in McDonald's with the time it would take to prepare the food and consume it. Predictability and consistency are also important. Wherever McDonald's operates, identical products and service are available. Finally, the system promotes control through the substitution of non-human technology for human activity.

> The humans who work in fast food restaurants are trained to do a very limited number of things in precisely the way they are told to do them. Managers and inspectors make sure that the workers toe the line. The human beings who eat in fast food restaurants are also controlled, albeit usually more subtly and indirectly. Lines, limited menus, few options, and uncomfortable seats all lead diners to do what the management wishes them to do – eat quickly and leave. Further, the drive through and in some cases walk-through window leads diners to first eat rapidly and then leave.[38]

Ritzer sees this leading to dehumanisation during the eating process (due to the resemblance to an assembly line), and to destruction of valuable cultural diversity because of this global 'mass' cuisine. Moreover, it raises the question of the reality of our 'version' of the past and what the future will actually mean. How far are we prepared to sacrifice our humanity to the logic of science?

BIOTECHNOLOGY AND THE RISK SOCIETY

Genetically engineered food products have been claimed to hold the promise of solving the food problems of the world. For opponents, they epitomise the *Risikogessellschaft* – incalculable consequences masquerading as progress and mastery over nature.[39]

In the UK, the Polkinghorne Committee,[40] which reported on ethical aspects of foods involving genetic modification, found no grounds to justify any general ethical prohibition on genetically modified organisms (GMOs) in food, but recommended that, in view of the possible religious dietary sensitivities involved in using animal or human copy genes, or their use in plants or micro-organisms where they would not be expected, there should be labelling to that effect. The use of human copy genes will be regulated to discourage the use of such ethically sensitive material in food production. Most people feel that consumers need more information in order to decide whether to use these foods or not. But, as we have seen, the erstwhile authority of science is compromised. How, then, will decisions be taken?

Cultural theory tells us that different groups will interpret information according to their prevailing values. Rather than simply being related to an evaluation or choice process restricted to one product, with judgement taking place on an 'objective' or 'value-free' basis, information is actually marshalled in order to place food within a broader perspective. Unsurprisingly, attitudes towards food cannot be formed in isolation from related attitudes and values. The same information, consequently, may well be used by different groups in order to sustain quite different positions.

It is perfectly feasible for committed animal rights activists to view every positive endorsement by scientists as biased and selective interpretation, just as food retailers will seize on the same message to confirm their faith in the safety of new products. Information is always interpreted according to pre-existing 'worldviews', and it is extremely difficult to challenge or change the core values upon which these rest. Food habits do not stand by themselves, but are part of a structured perception of the world. To challenge the meaning and role of food products and their usage within a form of life may well endanger fundamental aspects of the worldview of individuals concerned.

Cultural theory sees individuals as the active organisers of their own perceptions who choose what to fear, and how much to fear it, in order to support their way of life. Selective attention is paid to risk and preferences among different types of risk-taking/avoiding, according to 'cultural biases' (worldviews or ideologies entailing deeply held values and beliefs defending different patterns of social relations).[41] Views vary according to the type of social relations and the social order endorsed by the subject. The egalitarian, for example, sees nature as exploited and under threat by technology and science, since nature's resources are scarce and there is a tendency for the powerful to take more than their share; while the hierarchist sees the order and control involved as a good thing, as progress, as necessary and desirable. 'Fact' here will always be subordinate to cultural value.

Postmodern eating, then, seems likely to involve food habits in which culture plays just as large a part as in the past. Now, however, consumers are likely to be extremely self-conscious about how the food which they consume relates to the society which produced it, and to be influenced by ethical choices concerning production processes, the context of production and consumption, and the meaning and relevance of the food for the individual and others in the world.

NORMATIVE DIMENSIONS

Yet the normative issues involved seem particularly intractable. How are we to resolve the thorny ethical issues surrounding matters of public policy? As we have seen, genetic engineering raises issues which have yet to be satisfactorily addressed. GATT regulations mean that it is only the nature of the food, and not the process by which it was produced, which constitutes grounds on which importation of food products can be legally refused. Yet cultural differences mean that genetically modified food products may very well be unacceptable to large sections of a particular national population. German policy-makers, for example, believe they lag behind France and Britain in genetic technology because research has been hindered by strict legal regulations and public opposition, which has put off investors. Some federal states, particularly Hesse and North Rhine-Westphalia, have been criticised for supporting campaigns against genetic technology and for 'poisoning the climate for investment'. One estimate has it that although 40,000 people were employed in biotechnology in Germany, there could be in excess of 100,000 more jobs but for the uncertainty within the industry.[42] Despite the undoubted importance of this area in the future, the lack of domestic industrial interest in genetic technology has meant that publicly funded German scientists did research instead for the US and Japanese markets. Clearly, ethical considerations are still vitally important in a country which has often been seen as single-minded to the point of obsession in its pursuit of economic success.

In Britain, ethical dilemmas related to animal welfare have assumed prominence. Much-trumpeted campaigns against the cruelty of intensive farming and animal exports stand in contrast to the continued exemption of religious slaughter, as in 'halal' butch-ery,[43] from the regulations governing the humane treatment of farm animals. This may seem like simple expediency and venality on the part of those concerned in the food industry, but ethical standards here, as elsewhere, are not self-evident.

According to some radical commentators, the romanticisation and anthropomorphism which underlie many of the attitudes towards nature found in postmodern western societies, disillusioned with progress and frightened by the future, signify a decayed and self-absorbed western imperialist culture. 'Green' politics, vegetarianism, and animal welfare are part of 'new age' ethics which still fails to take seriously the experiences and concerns of groups which have been outside of western cultural history. The 'Grand Recits' of western ideas still exclude the 'Petit Recits' of outsiders and the weak.[44]

This nostalgic and conservative response of our society to the collapse of the industrial order represents a crisis of confidence in, and a deep disillusionment with, the project of modernity, and a recognition and critique of the individualistic, ethno- and phallocentric ethics of the Enlightenment which has always underlain that project. As Seyla Benhabib comments:

> The claim that the gender blindness of universalist theories is not merely a matter of moral indifference, or political inclination, but that it points to a deeper epistemic failure has been one of the cornerstones of the postmodernist critique of the grand narratives of the logocentric western tradition. If there is one commitment which unites postmodernists from Foucault to Derrida to Lyotard it is this critique of western rationality as seen from the perspective of the margins, from the standpoint of what and whom it excludes, suppresses, delegitimises, renders mad, imbecilic or childish.[45]

For Benhabib, the only way forward is to accommodate within the 'superliberalism', which much postmodernist thinking proposes, the 'petit recits' of 'women, children, fools and primitives', as Lyotard calls them, excluded by the 'grand narrative' of the enlightenment and its grandiose vision of the modernising of the west.

This must mean opening up the policy-making process to more varied ideas, and not embracing, uncritically, agendas born of culturally supremacist assumptions, however well meaning. This process must start early. Assumptions about the 'natural' way to think and feel about food are being formed in the home and school from the very beginning of life. The notion that diversity and variety are natural, that there are innumerable ways to think about food, are simply never introduced into our experience, yet they are fundamental to the development of civilised relations between culturally diverse groups. Ethical education in these matters can make a huge contribution to social harmony in the future.

NOTES

1   Beck, U. (1990) 'From industrial society to risk society: questions of survival, social structure and ecological enlightenment', *Theory, Culture and Society* 9, 97–123.

2   Robertson Smith, W., *The Religion of the Semites* (Edinburgh, Black, 1889).

3   Van Gennep, A., *The Rites of Passage* (Paris, Noury, 1960).

4   Ewart Evans, G., *Ask the Fellows Who Cut the Hay* (London, Routledge & Kegan Paul, 1950).

5   See: Harrison, T., *The Pub and the People: a worktown study by Mass Observation* (London, Redwood, 1943); Dennis, N., Henriques, F. and Slaughter, C., *Coal is Our Life* (London, Routledge, 1959); Gofton, L. (1983) 'Real men, real ale', *New Society* 66, 1096, 271–3; Gofton, L. (1988) 'Folk devils and the demon drink: drinking rituals and social integration in North East England', *Drogalkohol, Alkohol und Drogen* 12, 181–196.

6   Sen, A. (1981) 'Ingredients of famine analysis: availability and entitlements', *Quarterly Journal of Economics* XCVI, 3, 433–464.

7   Gellner, E., *Nations and Nationhood* (London, Routledge, 1982).

8   Douglas, M., *Purity and Danger* (Harmondsworth, Pelican, 1966).

9   Codere, H., *Fighting with Property* (London, Prentice Hall, 1971).

10   Mintz, S., *Sweetness and Power* (New York, Penguin, 1985).

11   See: Svenbro, J. (1984) 'The division of meat in classical antiquity', paper presented at a Symposium on Food Sharing, Bad Homburg, Germany, December 12; Detienne, M. (1977) 'La Viande et la Sacrifice en Grece Ancienne', *La Recherche*, February, 75, 152–160.

12   Elias, N., *The Civilizing Process* (2 vols), *Vol. 1: The History of Manners* (London, Blackwell, 1978).

13   Mennell, S. (1987) 'On the civilizing of appetite', *Theory, Culture and Society* 4(3–4), 373–403.

14   Elias, N., *The Court Society* (London, Blackwell, 1980).

15   Bauman, Z. (1983) 'Industrialism, consumerism and power', *Theory, Culture and Society* 1(3), 48–59.

16   Walton, J.K., *Fish and Chips and the British Working Class, 1870-1940* (Leicester, Leicester University Press, 1992).

17   See: Pearson, G., *Hooligan: a history of fears* (Oxford, Blackwell, 1983); Cohen, S., *Folk Devils and Moral Panics* (London, Paladin, 1970); Schwartz Cowan, R., *More Work for Mother: the ironies of household technology from the open hearth to the microwave* (London, Free Association Books, 1989).

18   Gershuny, J., Miles, I., Joes, S., Mullings, C., Thomas, G. and Wyatt, S. (1986) 'Time Budgets: preliminary analysis of a survey', *Quarterly Journal of Social Affairs* 2(1), 13–39.

19   National Food Survey (London, HMSO, 1995).

20   See: Gofton, L. (1995) 'Convenience and the moral status of convenience practices', in Marshall, D. (ed.) *Food Choice and the Consumer* (London, Blackie, 1995); Gofton, L. (1995) 'Dollar rich and time poor', *British Food Journal* (forthcoming).

21 Sennauer, A., Asp, E. and Kinsey, J., *Food Trends and the Changing Consumer* (Minnesota, Eagan Press, 1991).
22 See: Schwartz Cowan, 1989, op. cit.
23 See: Walton, 1992, op. cit.
24 Murcott, A. (1982) 'On the social significance of the cooked dinner in South Wales', *Social Science Information* 21(4/5), 677–695.
25 Charles, N., *Gender Divisions and Social Change* (Hemel Hempstead, Harvester, 1993).
26 Pahl, R. (1993) 'Rigid flexibilities? Work between men and women work', *Employment and Society* 7(4), 629–642.
27 See: Gershuny, J., *Social Innovation and the Division of Labour* (Oxford, Oxford University Press, 1983); Gershuny, J. and Jones, S., 'The changing work/leisure balance', in *Sport, Leisure and Social Relations* (Horne, J., Jary, E. and Tomlinson, P., eds) (London, Routledge & Kegan Paul, 1987), 9–50.
28 See: Pahl 1993, op. cit.
29 Falk, P., *The Consuming Body* (London, Sage, 1993).
30 Goffman, E., *Relations in Public* (Harmondsworth, Penguin, 1967).
31 Gofton, L. (1990) 'Food fears and time famines: some social aspects of choosing and using foods', in *Why We Eat What We Eat* (London British Nutrition Foundation Bulletin) 15(1) 79–95.
32 Beardsworth, A. (1990) 'Trans-science and moral panics: understanding food scares', *British Food Journal* 92, 5, 11–16.
33 Stephenson, P., *The Export of Live Farm Animals: a cruel trade that makes no economic sense*; and *The Welfare of Broiler Chickens* (Petersfield, Compassion in World Farming, 1995).
34 Thomas, K., *Man and the Natural World* (London, Allen Lane, 1985).
35 Elias, N. (1995) 'Technization and civilization', *Theory, Culture and Society* 12, 7–42.
36 Samuel, R., *Theatres of Memory* (London, Quarto, 1994).
37 Ritzer, G., *The McDonaldization of Society* (Thousand Oaks, Pine Forge Press, 1993).
38 Ibid.
39 Beck, U., *Organized Irresponsibility* (Polity Press, London, 1994); Beck, U., *The Risk Society* (London, Sage, 1992).
40 Report of the Committee on the Ethics of Genetic Manipulation of Food Use. MAFF (London, HMSO, 1993).
41 See: Wildavsky, A. and Dake, K. (1990) (Fall) 'Theories of Risk Perception', *Daedalus* 119(4), 41–60; Douglas, M., *Risk and Blame* (London, Routledge, 1992).
42 Brookman, J., 'Germany Gears Up for Biotech Top Spot', *Times Higher Education Supplement*, 20 October, 10.
43 'Halal' refers to animals prepared for cooking by means of slaughter which are ritualised and acceptable to Muslim religious beliefs. For example, animals are bled to death without first being stunned.
44 Benhabib, S., *Situating the Self* (Cambridge, Polity, 1991).
45 Ibid.

Chapter 9

Consumer sovereignty as ethical practice in food marketing

Robert Hamilton

In recent years, several aspects of food marketing have attracted debate which has a marked ethical spin. Two major aspects of the debate are: the use of additives in processed foods, and the intensive farming of animals and land. Both are complex, raising questions of the use of scientific evidence; consumer demand as leading, or led by, suppliers; the proper care of non-human animals and environment; and the quality of information offered to consumers.

This chapter looks at the ethics of these two sectors of food marketing: what is morally good and bad, whether there is a case for change and how things could improve.

APPLYING ETHICS TO FOOD MARKETING

Ethics in its fullness considers specific actions in concrete situations by identified actors. It is about a lived experience in its totality. In MacIntyre's words[1] it is 'a capacity to judge and to do the right thing in the right place at the right time and in the right way.' These tautological sounding words underline the highly concrete nature of ethics, a concreteness which can be grasped only partly in this chapter, because food marketing is here viewed in a general way, not as the specific actions of a manager, consumer or firm.

Acting ethically is an interplay of two different skills: abstract reasoning analysis (such as defining utilitarian costs and benefits, or defining rights) and skills in the intuitive feel of concrete experiences. 'Reasoning alone' writes Singer, 'proved incapable fully to resolve the clash between self interest and ethics'.[2] These are separate skills, so attempts to make an ethical judgements about a person's action by reason alone, as casuistry does, is to seek a 'will-o-the-wisp'.

This duality of abstract skills and clinical skills is not special to ethics. In management, the link between the abstract ideas of company plans and their clinical application in practice is a not a rational process. As Roethlisberger[3] describes it in his colourful way: 'you take the plan to Joe the supervisor with the intuitive skill to make it work'. Funtowicz and Ravetz[4] see 'knowing-that' (the abstract principles) and 'knowing-how' (the craft of doing) as different skills in science and administration. The craft skill of knowing-how is a genuine form of knowledge[5, 6] which is played down within the framework of rational decision-making, in part because it has an intuitive content. Funtowicz and Ravetz are close to Roethlisberger in using this term 'craft skill', though the latter makes a further distinction between the craft skill of a person who interacts with materials, for example, a painter, and the clinical judgement of a person responding to a social situation, for example, a manager choosing actions. Blanchard and Peale's three-point checklist to assess the ethical quality of a manager's choices brings together the abstract analysis and the intuitive feel of ethical actions: (i) is it legal? (ii) is it balanced between the parties? (iii) does it make the manager feel good about her/himself?[7]

THE SCOPE OF THIS CHAPTER

This chapter cannot be a full ethical examination of concrete actions. It examines ethical principles appropriate to marketing, offering a guiding framework (like car headlights) with which managers can make ethical judgements, that is, apply their clinical judgement to a situation, just as a physician has the guiding ethical framework of the Hippocratic oath for diagnosis and choice of treatments. It attempts to answer the question: is it possible to use general ethical principles to find a guiding framework for a manager in judging clinically how to market food ethically? It uses the three ethical principles of Marketing suggested by Craig Smith,[8] to see how they can be used to formulate a guiding framework for the food marketer. Other authors have offered ethical analysis for marketers[9, 10] but Craig Smith's principles balance generality (can be applied to any market) with specificity (can be of practical use) better than most.

THE PRACTICE OF CONSUMER SOVEREIGNTY

Craig Smith's three general ethical principles define consumer sovereignty, the ultimate ideal or 'Hippocratic oath' of Marketing. They are:

1 The target consumer should have the *capability* to understand the product and the risks.
2 The consumer, should have a *choice* of goods, provided by competition.
3 The consumer should have *information* sufficient to judge how expectations of the goods are satisfied.

These principles describe the content of consumer sovereignty, the aim, *telos* or standard of excellence of Marketing. They are deontological principles crafted to fit Marketing, in contrast to universal principles, for example of human rights or of truth telling, which fit all situations. Because they are special to Marketing and are internal goals of the practice of Marketing, in MacIntyre's sense of internal goals, they are the goals of the virtuous marketing manager.[11]

These three principles could be delineated more specifically in, say, a code of practice which would be appropriate to a specific field of Marketing, a product market such as food or shoes, or a service market such as dry cleaning or advertising. A few examples will illustrate what the terms capability, choice and information can mean in the field of food marketing. The examples move from the general principles towards the specific field of clinical judgement. The nearer to the concrete situation, the greater is the complexity; so there is some of my viewpoint and my intuitive feel in these examples.

The capability to reckon the risk to consumers is a major ingredient of the debate about additives. Consumers eating foods containing additives do not have the capability to understand the toxicological assessment of risks to their health. They are more likely to be capable of knowing if a food is acceptable to religious or moral principles such as vegetarianism, organic diets or Islam. Untutored consumers will not be capable of avoiding the risk of a food with artificial flavours if, as in the UK, the regulations specify that the label says 'flavour' for the artificial and 'flavoured' for the genuine, for example, 'blueberry flavour' or 'blueberry flavoured'. This is a wonderful example of logically defensible regulations misleading consumers; how the skills and integrity of the drafters contribute to the ethics of such a regulation is not explored in this paper.

Choice is assumed to be provided if there is competition, though this is not a simple matter. The principle of choice requires managers to want and to seek competition so that cornering a market, a monopoly, too protected a segmentation, or too niche a niche, would be excluded. An example of this is the debate in the UK on the local monopolies of some national supermarkets. Competition may however threaten the viability of a market, as the UK doorstep deliverers of milk have argued for many years against the Office of Fair Trading's endeavours to stop their price fixing.[12] A common argument is that consumers who want organic foods, or additive-free foods, are not given choice in the UK today, for the supply of these foods is very restricted. Some supermarkets respond to that lack by working to offer more of these foods by encouraging supplies to expand. Supermarket standardisation can restrict choice. The warm UK 1994 autumn produced smaller, less white cauliflowers than usual, which the supermarkets refused to buy as they were undersized and the wrong colour. There are consumers who would be pleased to buy this 'second class' produce, as they would be able in a distribution system of wholesalers and small retailers.

The claim that suppliers are working to improve choice widens the principle of choice to include the dynamics of competition over time and the credibility of the effort to change the market. In the European food market, the Common Agricultural Policy profoundly affects supply, so its aims and impact come under ethical scrutiny if the dynamics of competition are part of choice in the market. For example, the policy of set aside does less to increase consumer choice than would encouraging organic production, and on that basis an ethical manager in the food market would act to have the policy changed.

Debate on the quality of information about the product is a frequent irritant between managers and consumer critics. While no one defends straightforward lies and misrepresentations, the debate about the use of words such as 'natural', 'low fat', 'recommended retail price' and so on, are endless. The Advertising Standards Authority (ASA) criticised nutritional claims in February 1994, pointed out the potential for misleading consumers in the comparative pricing of baskets of foods in November 1994, and upheld three complaints of misleading nutritional information in an advertisement by the Butter Council in February 1995.

The ASA's judgements and commentaries are very helpful ethical guides, for with a detailed code and investigatory system, it tries to get as close as an outsider can to an ethical judgement of the situation as experienced by the actors. Using Blanchard and Peale's checklist, the ASA examines the legality and the balance of the argument between the parties, but it does not scrutinise the integrity of the parties, or how they feel about themselves in their actions. Advertising is a popular dump for annoyance and anger, so these cloud an assessment of the intentions moulding the complaints, which at times say more about the complainer than the advertisment.

As with all deontological principles, the interpretation of Craig Smith's three general guidelines for marketing is never definitive. This ambiguity does not exclude them from use as ethical guidelines, and here they are applied to three aspects of food marketing: food additives, intensive farming and the use of chemicals in modern farming.

THE SAFETY OF ADDITIVES IN FOODS

Additives have many functions in food manufacture on a large scale. They colour foods and recolour foods denuded by the manufacturing process, to make them attractive; make the ingredients easier to use on a mass scale; preserve foods from infection and oxidation; add nutrients and sweeteners; and keep the foods stable. There has been a very substantial expansion in their use in the last 40 years.

The main challenge to using additives is that expert opinion and a large proportion of consumers (up to 65% in national opinion surveys) view them as a health risk, as inducing acute adverse reactions (e.g. rashes, hyperactivity) in some people and chronic reactions (e.g. cancer, kidney, gene damage) in others. There is also the less frequent challenge, not covered in this chapter, that additives encourage the manufacture of attractive food of low nutritional quality, i.e. junk foods, and a poor diet.

Assessing the safety of additives is a role of the UK government which holds many challenges for the regulators. The fundamental problem is that the three assessment techniques available provide uncertain and unreliable evidence. One, human epidemiology, cannot obtain the large samples needed or the fine texture of the data to identify a risk; a second, *in vitro* testing, has a very limited scope; and the third, *in vivo* testing on non-human animals, carries too heavy a burden of extrapolation across species.[13–16]

Evidence of acute adverse reactions in humans is disputed. From research so far, the proportion of the population harmed is tiny, and the human experience, for example, rashes, nausea, dizziness, hyper-activity, asthma and stomach pains, are not of the type detected in laboratory experiments on animals. This is not just a scientific dispute, as the commercial needs for competitive edge and legal protection are involved, causing ambiguity about values of openness and objective rigour of science and of consumer satisfaction and competition in marketing. Evidence of adverse chronic reactions is absent. Mansfield[17] argues 'common sense alone forces us to the conclusion that continuous doses of a cocktail of 4,000 chemicals, amounting to ½ ounce a day, must be doing at least some people appreciable harm'.

There are three ways of creating a response to this situation, which I classify as: (1) free market, (2) scientific regulation, and (3) cultural symbolism. These are beliefs about what reality is, and Craig Smith's principles of marketing ethics can be applied to each one.

Free market

The free market view is that competition will eliminate the dangers and define the risk acceptable to consumers. This outcome requires that firms give ready access to data on safety and on use of additives, and that consumers have time and knowledge to understand the data; the lack of data on chronic adverse effects is ignored. Both of these are highly unlikely. Aside from these impracticalities, this view of the situation upholds to some degree all three of Craig Smith's principles. Competition gives choice, consumers capable of understanding risk, and information to assess how the product meets their expectations about additives. However, this only looks like a quality ethical response to the anxiety about additives, for it is thoroughly imprac-tical. It would be a defensible position if the danger were defined as not existing (as government ministers nearly do at times[18]), or as less than other dangers accepted by consumers, for example, allergies caused by traditional foods (as firms, civil servants and scientists do[19]).

Scientific regulation

Scientific regulation involves the use of scientific procedures to assess the safety and regulate the use of additives. This is the view of the situation taken officially by governments and described in the official brochures offered to the public. Results of scientific tests are assessed by committees of experts, who pronounce on the safety of the additive taking account of the current consumption of foods likely to contain it. Additives which pass through this process are deemed safe, possibly with details of permitted use, and a statement of Acceptable Daily Intake. Confirmation of the assessed safety is made available to consumers via a labelling system, for example, E numbers. The labels are useful to consumers who seek to avoid specific additives but of little use to anyone else, for example, those who seek to keep intake within some acceptable limits, or those not alerted to the risks.

A more fundamental problem than labelling is the inability of the science of toxicology to give valid information on safety. Regulation can design the best that is on offer, via codes of good laboratory practice, but has a limited credibility. Even at its best, in the saccharin debacle in the 1970s, science was subjected to public ridicule. Led by the low-calorie drink firms, the USA public derided the conclusion of a high-quality *in vivo* study that the data on rats extrapolated to humans implied a danger of cancer from a consumption of 800 cans of Coca Cola a day![20] No matter how this regulatory process is honed – for example by ensuring good laboratory practice, and placing consumer representatives on the committees of experts – the un-certainty and unreliability of the tests are not improved because the basic idea, that a non-human mammal's response can replicate a human's response, is flawed. This invalidity is compounded when experts use aggregated data of food consumption to assess whether the, unreliable, Acceptable Daily Intake is likely to be breached by consumers. As there is little medical research into additives, it is left to consumers to find out by trial and error whether they are acutely challenged by any additive, though often when a consumer makes a diagnosis it is disputed on the grounds that there is no scientific evidence of the response.

This scientific regulation of additives has low ethical quality; for it upholds, in a weak way, only two of the ethical principles: the consumer has choice (via competition), and information to assess whether the product meets expectations (via E numbers on labels). The capability of understanding the risk by consumers or the regulators, as consumer advisors, is low. This is not a criticism of toxicology as a science but of its use by regulators who want what it cannot give. Thus, Whittemore[21] quotes a US FDA Commissioner: 'I'm looking for a clean bill of health, not a wishy-washy, iffy answer on cyclamates'. Nor is it a judgement on politicians who act intuitively in a context of unpredictability and unreliability, where political survival is the objective and the task an art not a science. The information is assessed pragmatically: 'will it help me win or deflect blame if I lose?'.[22] It is a criticism of being dishonest with oneself and others about how one sees things, of being economical with one's truth, and of a corrupt use of science.

Cultural symbolism

The cultural view sees the situation as one of consumer anxiety, based upon socio-psychological factors, requiring a symbolic response to allay anxiety. Scientific proof of dangers or safety is not needed in this view, so, while the authenticity of the scientific rituals is important, it is free of the unending debate on the minutiae of toxicological evidence. Science is used for its symbolic value in popular culture, as a source of truth. The scientific symbols of well designed laboratory experiments, committees of independent experts, and technical language (e.g. No Effect Levels, Acceptable Daily Intake) are used to design a ritual which gives a credible authority to the outcome of the process, for example, a permitted list, which can allay anxieties of consumers, manufacturers and the government. As well as the symbols, secrecy is an ingredient of this process, to avoid a debate in terms of scientific realism which would be hostile to the cultural beliefs with which the process is defined.

With this symbolic view of the situation, the first two of Craig Smith's principles are upheld, but only weakly, viz. choice, from competition, and the information to assess how expectations are satisfied, from a labelling scheme. Capability needs redefinition, from understanding objective risks to allaying subjective anxieties in a situation of irredeemable objective uncertainty. If that were the case, the principle of capability would be honoured.

Summary

The ethical quality of each response is different. In the free market approach there is an unreal ethical quality, for its assumptions about openness of information and the capability of consumers to use it are idealised and unattainable. In scientific regulation, a definition of reality dominant today, there is an ethical defect of claiming knowledge of safety when, on scientific criteria, it does not exist. In cultural symbolism, a post-modern view of reality, it has the highest ethical quality – but this is likely to be criticised as corrupt and dishonest from the predominant modernist, scientific belief system in which intellect and fact are given much greater reverence than feeling and ritual. Hence, a manager does not often feel free to choose this reality.

PRODUCTION OF FOOD BY INTENSIVE FARMING

This is a more complex issue than the safety of additives and there are many more loose ends. The food most people eat is produced by systems in farms and in large-scale manufacture and retailing that claim to provide desirable efficiencies and low prices. The farm systems are the centre of debate about the treatment of non-human animals, for example, hens in cages, chickens and turkeys in broiler units, calves in crates, pigs in stalls, and about the effects on the ecosystem of monoculture, for example, soil erosion, wildlife habitat depletion, pollution, and the adverse effects on human health of residues of chemical fertilisers, growth hormones and pesticides. Genetic engineering adds complexity to all these.

The ethical debate has three strands: the treatment of non-human animals, degradation of the ecosystem and risks to human health. The first and second go beyond the individual to society and the ecosystem, which are outside the scope of Craig Smith's principles. The maltreatment of animals may be linked to personal cruelty, thus extending the risks to society, as well as involving the loss of the psychic talents of animals as, for example, healers, teachers and seers.[23-25] Like the risk to the ecosystem, society, and not the individual, bears the extended risk. Craig Smith's principles are within a modernist, rational-individualist view of reality, different from the reality of these systemic risks. Individuals can make effective choices about risks to personal health and their treatment of animals, but one person cannot change a system. A majority of individuals could influence change, but are unlikely to make the choices which effect change when the culture gives low value to the ecosystem and to the lives of non-human animals, and the related economic costing externalises the degradation. For example, the demand for competitively priced cow's milk places a low moral value upon the life of a calf, so that it can be removed from the cow and reared in a narrow crate. Adults of one species drinking the food for babies of another species is doubly odd biologically, but culturally encouraged. The Meat and Livestock Commission's promotional policy of diverting consumers' awareness away from the production process (the consumers do not want to know') uses economic resources to sustain a state of consumer ignorance. 'Let the polluter pay' is a good individualist principle, but it is often difficult to know who the polluter is, so the costs of cleanup, or of identifying who is responsible, are excluded from the polluter's costing.

Green consumerism is an individual's response to social and ecosystem risks, but it has an insecure role in the market. It quickly moves into the debate on the basis of values contrasting a superficial anthropocentrism to a deep, Gaia-centred greenness. For the latter, humans are a contributor to the inter-related wholeness of the planet, not its dominant managers. A Gaia-centred society, which is likely to have a majority being vegetarian or eating only organic foods, would have a worldview in which the individualistic consumer satisfaction of modern societies would have an insecure place.

Marketing ethics, animal welfare and ecosystem conservation

Consumers are free to make choices about these issues. There are limits to consumer sovereignty (for example, they cannot choose illegal products) but neither the differences of opinion about the treatment of animals and about the care of the ecosystem in farming, nor the ineffectiveness of the actions of individual consumers, justify refusing consumers a choice of products. The marketing principle of capablity requires that information about methods of farming and production be available in considerable detail. The principle of information, to judge that what is bought is what is wanted (for example, 'vegan', 'organic'), reinforces the requirement. There is a strong expectation that sellers will provide this information. The debate about these issues, especially animal welfare, touches deep feelings which deter openness, and Marketing's impetuosity for telling an attractive story reinforces this defensiveness. (A reasoned and thorough account of the debate on animal welfare is possible and an excellent one is the Report of the House of Commons Committee on Agriculture of 1981.[26]) Precisely what and how much information is provided depends on the judgement of the marketing manager. It is a judgment which takes a position on elusive details, such as what consumers can understand, how to avoid the unreasonable attentions of pressure groups, and how much evidence to collect on production practices, consumers' attitudes and ethics, in order to inform the manager's choice. Craig Smith's principles challenge profoundly the promotional advocacy that is the habitual style in Marketing. Following Blanchard and Peale's ethical checklist, in that judgement marketing managers need to balance interests (and not be advocates merely of their own interests), and to maintain personal integrity, that is, to choose in a way that makes managers feel good about themselves.

The principle of choice places a requirement on the market to supply the preferred products. A firm does this by being competitive, avoiding monopolistic situations, and by being sensitive to consumer wants. In the food market, many of the firms are very large (for example, supermarkets, Unilever, Procter and Gamble, United Biscuits, Nestlé, the Co-op) and they are greatly challenged to supply small segments of the market that animal welfare and conservation interests bring into being. They also face the temptation to block entry of small firms into the mainstream market. Health food shops and organic food distributors serve a small adventurous segment and mainstream firms and supermarkets are tempted to 'steal' their successful lines, as in the case of muesli in the 1980s, without acknowledging economically these shops' innovative efforts. The managers of large firms can experience their jobs as responding to consumer wants in a competitive world, while seekers of vegetarian and organic foods reasonably claim that their wants are poorly served.

The inertia built into size and competitive advantage makes it difficult for managers to take a lead in developing niche products, and too easy to make a judgement not to take a lead. The principle of choice gives the large firm the task of either leading or of fostering competition. Kelloggs, whose strengths are in big, fine technology and large market segments, would have found muesli an awkward product when the demand was small, in the 1970s and 1980s, for muesli is very low technology: anyone can mix bags of cereals, nuts and fruits. Organic breakfast cereals, which might have appealed to Kelloggs in the early days of the firm, have too limited a supply and too small a demand for the firm today. A marketing tactic difficult to justify under the principle of choice would be to block the super-market shelves with the firm's token version of the niche product, unsupported by promotion, as an obstacle to both competition and market penetration.

CHEMICAL RESIDUES IN FOOD

The evidence that intensive farming produces low-quality food is still elusive, so I want to focus here on the more certain dangers from residues of chemicals used in today's farming. The essence of the matter is in the report of the House of Commons Agriculture Committee in 1986:

> Having studied the detailed memoranda and heard oral evidence, we have concluded that anxiety about pesticides can no longer be allayed by merely stating that no harmful effects have been observed and that therefore pesticides are safe. Those responsible must convince the public that they have knowledge, resources and independent judgement, and they must do this in a more open way.[27]

There are close parallels here with the position on additives. Information on safety is not available and consumers are not capable of understanding the risks. The Agriculture Committee sees the regulators as adopting a cultural symbolic approach under the guise of scientific regulation.

In the UK the burden of toxicological testing and formulating good farming practice in using products is placed upon the chemical firms, while the government regulates the testing and collects data on residues. The problems of extrapolating results in laboratory mammals to humans creates uncertainty, though there is a greater chance of detecting acute effects on humans from pesticides than from additives. Changes in data collection on residues in the past decade, involving for example, more samples and measuring residues in crops instead of in a typical meal, have found higher residues. Increases in permitted residue levels have been possible as there is uncertainty about toxicity. The commercial interests of chemical companies and the attitudes of a government with a strong preference for deregulation will be challenged to find the balanced, objective position on the collection and dissemination of the data that the Commons Committee wants.

With such uncertainty, secrecy on information, plus some ritualistic collection of data and meetings of expert committees, is the way chosen in the UK to allow farmers to use xenobiotic chemicals that improve commercial productivity while keeping consumers sanguine. This is how additives are regulated – by employing a set of rituals, portrayed as scientific procedures, that sustains consumer confidence in the market. If the process is viewed as using cultural symbols to produce a socio-psychological effect, then the principle of capability, redefined as allaying consumer anxieties, is honoured.

Information about pesticides used or about the residues present on the food in the shops is almost non-existent beyond the dichotomy of none used (organic) or some used. Advice is provided about washing and preparing some fresh foods, which is of limited help in avoiding the toxins. *WHICH?* magazine found the claims of some commercial washes to remove residues to be invalid and there needs to be a high frequency or high level of residues to persuade the government to broadcast advice on food preparation, as it does with carrots. It is a daunting task to channel information to consumers. Accurate records on pesticides used would need to accompany food through the distribution chain. So, it is tempting to argue that the consumers do not need the information and to sustain their lack of awareness of a likely risk by not mentioning it, as the government did by keeping quiet about the level of residues of Alar, a pesticide, in apple juices in 1995.

Apart from the limited availability of organic foods, consumers have a highly restricted choice of foods with no residues, or preferred types of them, as in the rare case of Jordan's conservation grade cereals. Use of chemicals is so widespread in farming and food production that there is a clear case, based on the principle of choice, for firms in the market to foster alternatives; to take a lead as, for example, the supermarket chain Safeway does in organic farming, and to put force into government agencies which work to regulate and reduce the risks from chemicals in the food chain.

In this area, of the risk to human health from pesticides in food, none of the three principles of Marketing is honoured. The consumer is not capable of understanding the risks, very little information is available on the presence of residues in foods, and there is a highly restricted choice.

CONCLUDING SUMMARY

The ethical quality of Marketing is not high in the fields of food marketing examined here: additives; animal welfare and ecosystem care; and pesticide residues. There are common features why this is so.

In all three fields, competition is naively relied on to provide choice. This will happen only when there is avoidance of the negative consequences, such as over-strong competition, which removes competitors or leads to cartels; or of the difficulty for oligopolistic firms to serve small segments or to foster small firms that could. UK law on monopolies and restrictive practices regulates the over-strong competition, but it does not, nor could, animate firms to want and seek out competition, which is the essence of Marketing. The ethical quality of a firm's choices in supporting and enhancing consumer choice can be assessed by the extent that competition is actively sought. Merely to obey the anti-trust laws is the minimum of marketing ethics.

Information is needed by consumers to be able to judge if the product is as expected. In the market sectors examined information is absent on product safety, is absent or veiled about the effects on the ecosystems and is veiled from consumers on animal welfare. This is far from the essence of good Marketing, the sovereignty of the consumer, which enjoins the firm and manager to be an open channel of information about the product, and avoid being just an advocate of the seller's interests.

This is a challenging task, for it will take time for consumers to learn to deal with information about risks in a mature, balanced way, and firms will need help from outside to become more open. A good example of such help is the WHO International Code of Marketing of Breast-milk Substitutes.[28] Drafted with the help of medical professionals, governments and interest groups, it contains in detail what information mothers should have, as well as guidance on marketing, that is, advertising, samples and sponsorship. An assessment of the ethical quality of a firm would include the extent to which it actively wants and seeks to provide information to consumers. The absence of such a desire creates a context in which managerial choices are likely to be of low ethical quality.

The capability of the consumers to understand the risks in the market sectors examined is small. For additive and pesticide safety and ecosystem damage this inability reflects a universal lack of knowledge; for animal welfare, consumers have a low awareness of the treatment of animals on farms and there is scant understanding of the positive talents of non-human animals in the ecosystem or as companions. On consumer safety, Marketing needs to be circumspect. Absence of understanding should prescribe a miserly use of products with a potential danger. The enthusiasm shown by food scientists for their novel tastes and textures, created with the help of additives, is discrepant with high-quality marketing ethics; the genetic development of crop types that can take higher doses of pesticides should evoke wariness in the Marketing Manager; and in the vigorous promotion of BST (bovine somatotrophin) we see Marketing using zealous advocacy when the prescription is for miserly circumspection.

This view of sectors of Food Marketing in the light of Craig Smith's principles of Consumer Sovereignty has arrived at a picture of a firm with high-quality ethics as enthusiastic for competition, wanting openness with information and promoting products with precautionary circumspection. This will be challenging for firms because it is counter to the exuberant advocacy of Marketing and to the concealment of information in the Food Market.

The picture testifies to the ethical status of a firm but not to every choice of its managers. Within a firm with such qualities, a manager will find rational and emotional support for choices that are ethically of high quality.

NOTES

1   MacIntyre, A., *After Virtue* 2nd edn (London, Duckworth, 1985) p.150.
2   Singer, P., *How Are We To Live?* (Melbourne, The Text Publishing Company, 1993) p.262.
3   Roethlisberger, F.J., *The Elusive Phenomena* (Boston, Harvard University Press, 1977).
4   Funtowicz, S.O. and Ravetz, J.R. *Uncertainty and Quality in Science for Policy* (Dordrecht, Kluwer Academic Publishers, 1990) p.60.
5   Pirsig, R., *Zen and the Art of Motorcycle Maintenance* (New York, Bantam, 1974).
6   Polanyi, M. *Personal Knowledge* (London, Routledge & Kegan Paul, 1958).
7   Blanchard, K. and Vincent Peale, N., *The Power of Ethical Management* (London, Cedar Books, 1988) p.139.
8   Craig Smith, N. in *Ethics in Marketing*, Craig Smith, N. and Quelch, J.A. (eds) (Boston MA, Irwin, 1993) p.838.
9   Laczniak, G.R. (1983) 'Framework for analysing marketing ethics', *Journal of Macromarketing* Spring: 7.
10 Baumaol, W.J. and Blackman, S.A.B., *Perfect Markets and Easy Virtue: business ethics and the invisible hand*, Mitusi Lectures in Economics, Winters, L.A. (ed.) (Cambridge, Mass., Blackwell, 1991) p.134.
11 MacIntyre, 1985, op. cit.
12 OFT (1994) 'Price-fixing in door-step milk', *Fair Trading* Spring.
13 Conning, D.M., Leigh, L. and Ricketts, B.D. 'How to survive food marketing: see through the tinsel and the hype and do your own thing', in *Food Fit to Eat* (London, Sphere Books, 1988).
14 Rowan, A.N., *Of Mice, Models and Men* (New York, University of New York Press, 1984).
15 Millstone, E. and Abraham, J., *Additives: a guide for everyone* (Harmondsworth, Penguin, 1988).
16 Millstone, E., *Food Additives: taking the lid off what we really eat* (Harmondsworth, Penguin, 1986).
17 Mansfield, P. and Munro, J., *Chemical Children* (London, Century, 1987).

18 Cannon, D., *The Politics of Food* (London, Century, 1986) pp.148–157.
19 Richmond, C. (1986) 'Food additives? No problem', *New Scientist* 13 February, 56.
20 Feldman, L.P., 'Science politics and the regulation of food and drug safety', 5th ESSEC Seminar, *Marketing and Public Policy* (France, ESSEC Cergy-Pontoise, 1979) pp.167–185.
21 Whittemore, A.S. (1983) 'Facts and values in risk assessment for environmental toxicants', *Risk Analysis* 3, 23.
22 Clark, W.C. and Majone, G. (1985) 'Critical appraisal of scientific inquiries with policy implications', *Science, Technology and Human Values* 10(3), 6.
23 Hall, R., *Animals are Equal: an exploration of animal consciousness* (London, Wildwood House, 1980).
24 Ferris, C., *The Darkness is Light Enough* (London, Sphere Books, 1986) p.404.
25 Birch, C., Eakin, W. and McDaniel, J.B. (eds), *Liberating Life. Contemporary Approaches to Ecological Theology* (New York, Orbis Books, 1991) p.293.
26 House of Commons, Agriculture Committee, *Animal Welfare in Poultry, Pig and Veal Calf Production* (London, House of Commons, 1981) 406-1, 406-2.
27 House of Commons, Agriculture Comittee, *Pesticide Safety in Agriculture*, Special Report (London, House of Commons, 1987). HC 379 I, II, III.
28 World Health Organisation, *International Code of Marketing of Breastmilk Substitutes* (Geneva, WHO, 1981).

Chapter 10

Ethical issues in agricultural and food research policy

Ben Mepham

INTRODUCTION

> Agricultural science has indeed transformed the practice of agriculture. Discoveries made by people in white coats ... have been transferred into farmers' fields in a bewilderingly short space of time, assisted by a wide network of institutions ... aimed at speeding up the process of technology transfer.[1]

Howard Newby's claim could be illustrated by countless examples. Characteristically, small numbers of scientists, through a combination of ingenuity and technical skill, and backed by adequate financial support, have devised technologies which have had profound and dramatic effects on society, the physical environment and trade on both national and international scales. The Green Revolution, involving the introduction of new high-yielding varieties of wheat and rice, is but one example of this revolutionary tendency.

So, science is powerful; and since technologies (applications of science) are capable of both use and abuse, the case for their ethical evaluation seems self-evident. But whether, and how, ethical considerations should impact on scientific research at the policy-making stage is by no means obvious. The aims of this chapter are twofold: to suggest that ethical evaluation *does* have an important role in research policy-making; and to propose a framework for addressing ethical issues. It does not seek to advance particular policies, but rather to make provocative challenges to accepted criteria in the interests of stimulating constructive dialogue.

Almost by definition, ethics can be said to be universal in scope, rational in procedure and impartial in outcome. But in order to address this issue in terms that are more concrete than abstract, it will be useful to consider policy questions raised in a specific sociopolitical context – and for current purposes the focus will be on agricultural and food research policy in the UK: the principles implicit in the analysis should, however, have wider applicability.

AGRICULTURAL POLICY IN THE UK

To examine the determinants of research policy we need first to consider the broader question of agricultural policy. Since the Second World War, government policy on agriculture has been largely shaped by the passage of the 1947 Agriculture Act, which aimed at the production of cheap and plentiful food. Although this legislation has been considerably revised and amended, particularly following Britain's entry into the European Community in 1973, the 'productionist paradigm',[2] as it has been called, has remained largely unchallenged, at least until very recently. Thus, the 1947 Agriculture Act presaged the advent of 'agribusiness', the profit-driven emphasis in agriculture which has been promoted and sustained by a stream of technological developments.

Until recently this quest for increased productivity was unproblematical. The rationale was simple. Increasing demands for land for housing, roads and industrial development; concerns for improved public health by providing nutritionally sound food at low prices; and farm workers' aspirations for a higher standard of living after the rigours of the war years – all these led to an increasing intensification of agricultural practice, that is, to an increased output of food per farm worker and per unit area of land. In ethical terms, the motive was essentially utilitarian.

Paul Thompson has suggested[3] that in North America, this drive for productivity is historically rooted in deep-seated metaphysical beliefs, such as the 'doctrine of grace', namely, that prolificacy was a sign of God's blessing, and the 'myth of the garden', which placed a moral obligation on farmers to tame and cultivate 'wild nature' for human benefit. Productionism, in such terms, was unquestionably 'good'. It would be surprising if such motives did not also apply in the UK, and, like the author, many readers may recall the unalloyed worthiness assigned to the harvest festivals of their childhood.

Latterly, however, this simplistic productionist objective, driven by yield-enhancing technologies, has been found wanting. Not only has it proved to be too successful, such that surplus yields have resulted in 'mountains' of beef and wheat and 'lakes' of milk and wine, but the technologies by which such increases in production have been achieved have been called into question for their pollutive and destructive effects on the environment, deleterious impacts on food safety, and adverse effects on rural employment and animal welfare. Moreover, Western consciences have been pricked by regular television portrayals of starving people in Africa at a time when, in Europe, 'intervention' permits food to remain in silos, or worse is allowed to rot, to maintain prices.

The political response to over-production has largely consisted of measures such as the imposition of quotas on milk production and enforced 'set aside' of land – downstream adjustments which ignore the productionist momentum of contemporary agricultural research.

AGRICULTURAL AND FOOD RESEARCH IN THE UK

It is implied above that there is strong link between what happens in the research laboratory and what happens in the agricultural and food industry. But the link need not, and in practice hardly ever does, conform to the so-called linear model. According to this, scientists, driven solely by the logic of their problem-solving curiosity, discover facts about the natural world, which if proved amenable to practical application are commercially exploited for the benefit of society at large. Clearly, modern science is far from such a disinterested pursuit of knowledge, and its evident power has led to attempts to direct it to specific ends for national or private benefit: hence, the importance of science policy.

Commenting on science policy in general, Webster recently identified four trends which are shaping the institutional character of science and technology. First, there has been a shift to interdisciplinary 'centres of excellence', allowing cost-effective use of expensive equipment and facilities; second, the distinction between 'science' and 'technology' has become blurred; third, scientific knowledge has become increasingly commercialised; and fourth, there is a growing social demand for the regulation and steering of science.[4] State-funded agricultural and food research in the UK demonstrates all four trends, which have resulted in a radical and almost continuous restructuring process over the last decade. Ethical implications of these four trends for research policy are discussed below.

Following publication of the government's White Paper 'Realising our Potential' in 1993,[5] the new Biotechnology and Biological Sciences Research Council (BBSRC) took over responsibility *inter alia* for the research previously administered by the Agricultural and

Food Research Council (AFRC). A principal aim of the council's activities is to 'identify and fund excellent science – basic, strategic and applied – that will contribute to the competitiveness of UK industries and improve the quality of life' and its research strategy is to 'seize new scientific opportunities as they arise (science push) and to respond to technological demands of industry (market pull).[6] In these objectives it is guided by the Technology Foresight Programme, which aims to bring together scientists and industrialists to identify markets and technologies likely to emerge over the next ten to twenty years.[7]

In order to facilitate exploitation of discoveries in basic science, the BBSRC has established three Directorates with the aim of ensuring that the needs of the various user communities are addressed, namely the Agricultural Systems (ASD), Food (FD), and Chemicals and Pharmaceuticals Directorates. Only the former two are relevant to this discussion. For example, currently, the management committee of the ASD, chaired by the deputy-president of the National Farmers Union, comprises fifteen members, who include farmers, research institute representatives, industry representatives, government department representatives, academics and a single representative of consumer interests.

Government-supported research is also carried out by the Ministry of Agriculture, Fisheries and Food (MAFF), which has an emphasis on applied rather than basic studies. Much of MAFF's strategic research is performed by scientists in BBSRC institutes or in universities, under the 'customer-contractor' principle.

In the commercial arena, there is considerable investment in research by food, agribusiness and pharmaceutical companies, and transnational corporations are particularly significant players in biotechnology and food processing research. At the other end of the scale, there are a few, small, privately funded research organisations, such as the Henry Doubleday Research Association and Elm Farm Research, which are concerned with the development of organic farming systems.

In the following discussion, the main focus will be on the research policies of the BBSRC, and to a lesser extent of those on MAFF,[8] since they are most clearly related to the public policy issues with which this volume is concerned.

ETHICS AND RESEARCH POLICY

That the word 'ethics' does not appear in the BBSRC's Corporate Plan or the MAFF Research Strategy is hardly surprising: after all, in conversation we do not constantly remind our listeners that we are telling the truth. But the omission might have a more substantive basis. Thus, it might be claimed that in democratic societies market forces will guarantee that consumers have opportunities for ethical choices, and that since ethical values within society are not uniform, all that is necessary is to ensure that the market *does* allow free and informed choices. Thereby, unethical practices will wither on the vine. The defects of this approach have been emphasised by other contributors to this book: in short, it is an approach which is undermined by the virtual impossibility of ensuring that consumers do have free and informed choices.

Another argument, which might be held to be consistent with the latter, is that science is impervious to ethical evaluation because it is concerned solely with the acquisition of 'facts' about the natural world, which in themselves have no moral implications. The claim is open to serious challenge in epistemological terms (the real nature of 'facts' is betrayed by the Latin origin, *facere*, meaning 'to make or do') but, in any case the view is undermined by the conflation of science and technology which is evident in the very title and aims of the BBSRC.

A more moderate defence of omitting reference to ethics might concede the importance of ethical concerns, but maintain that the commonly perceived relativity of ethical judgements and the notion that they are in any case subsumed by other considerations, such as public acceptability (which is addressed by public education pro-grammes), justifies omitting any specific reference to them.

Yet if, as implied by the power of science to so profoundly affect our lives, ethical issues *are* important, there is a strong case for explicit appeal to ethics in the formulation of research policy. Indeed, in recent years numerous committees have been set up to consider the ethics of biotechnological developments,[9] and it would be surprising, to say the least, if their conclusions were not relevant to research policy.

A major impediment to incorporating ethical concerns in science policy must surely be the cultural gap between the sciences and the humanities: it is a gap which can hardly be said to have been significantly narrowed since C.P. Snow famously described it in his 'Two Cultures' lecture nearly 40 years ago.[10] A crucial challenge for the bioethicist today is thus to propose a means of ethical analysis of biotechnological issues which commends itself as both comprehensible and reasonable to scientists, policy-makers and people in society as a whole.

One way of addressing ethical issues in a systematic way is to employ the 'ethical matrix' described in chapter 7. In brief, this seeks to define *prima facie* duties to respect certain principles (well-being, autonomy and justice) as they apply to the impacts of any technology on all affected interest groups (for example, consumers, producers, future generations, farm animals, the biotic environment). Thus, if a research policy is to be ethically appraised, the implications for a range of ethical principles, as they affect the various interest groups, will have to be put into the frame. It is stressed, as discussed in chapter 7, that the matrix is not prescriptive but provides a framework for rational and transparent policy decision-making. It is unlikely that any scientific or technological development could fully respect all the identified principles: nevertheless, it is important that all receive due consideration in policy formulation.

Now, two factors immediately become apparent if one adopts such a scheme of ethical auditing. First, many issues raised by this process are already addressed in the context of 'user community requirements' by current policies (for example, priorities are assigned to animal welfare and to food safety by the ASD and FD Strategies, respectively). But, second, many of the interest groups (for example, people in sub-Saharan Africa, unborn generations, farm animals) have no way of influencing research policy because they are not scientists, members of user communities (in the sense defined) or consumers expressing their preference through their purchasing power in the market. Despite this, their lives might be profoundly affected by implementation of new agricultural and food technologies.

Two types of ethical question thus arise, which can be characterised as acts of (1) omission and (2) commission, namely:

1 Can the omission from current research policy of issues which have an ethical dimension be justified?
2 Are those aspects of current research policy which have an ethical dimension being addressed in an ethically defensible manner?

A CRITIQUE OF CURRENT RESEARCH POLICY

Several caveats need to be issued before embarking on any discussion of research policy. First, the subject matter is inherently uncertain because of the propensity of science, by its very nature, to throw up new ideas unexpectedly. Second, in certain respects, the agricultural and food industries are subject to almost as much uncertainty as a result of political and economic change as is the growth of scientific knowledge itself. Third, the attainment of scientific expertise often involves a lengthy period of training for scientists and substantial expenditure on state of the art scientific equipment, so that targeting research to precise ends is not only difficult but in some cases undesirable. In short, futurology in science is an imprecise activity. But having said that, there are a number of issues bearing on food and agriculture over which there is little doubt.

Acts of omission

Consider the following:

- Substantial numbers of people in the world (between 0.5 and 1.0 billion) are seriously malnourished.
- The global population is set to almost double over the next 50 years, and the vast majority of that increase will be in parts of the world where most of the people already suffering from malnutrition live.
- Supplies of fossil fuels, which are essential for the intensive agriculture to which Western countries appear committed, are running out.
- Soil erosion is a significant problem in terms of future food productivity.[11]

From an impartial ethical viewpoint (and there can be no other sort) the omission of research directed to addressing such problems on a global scale represents a failure to respect the well-being of deprived people in less developed countries and of future generations more generally. It infringes this ethical principle because the UK government could direct more of its scientific resources to solving such problems; and in this context *could* implies *should*.

> Hunger is intolerable in the modern world in a way it could not have been in the past. This is not so much because it is more intense, but because widespread hunger is so unnecessary and unwarranted

in the modern world. The enormous expansion of productive power that has taken place over the last few centuries has made it, perhaps for the first time, possible to guarantee adequate food for all, and it is in this context that the persistence of hunger and the recurrence of virulent famines must be seen as being morally outrageous and politically unacceptable.[12]

Recognition of the human right to food has been constantly asserted in international agreements, for example in the UN Declaration of Human Rights and the International Convention on Economic, Social and Cultural Rights. Yet, in 1984, the 'foremost legal expert on food rights' was able to write:

> Few rights have been endorsed with such frequency, unanimity or urgency as the right to food, yet probably no other right has been as comprehensively and systematically violated on such a wide scale in recent decades.[13]

Of course, the missions of the BBSRC and MAFF implicitly ignore such issues: they are simply not within their remit. Indeed, with the reorganisation of the UK science base in 1993 all the research councils were charged with the primary objective of 'contributing to the competitiveness of UK industries and improving the quality of life'[14] (in the UK). This emphasis was made even more explicit in 1995 with the transfer of the Office of Science and Technology from the Office of Public Service and Science to the Department of Trade and Industry 'to allow the Government's policies on science, engineering and technology to be developed alongside its policies on industry'.[15]

The question of how much a country such as Britain is morally obligated to relieve the suffering of those abroad is discussed in chapter 1. But if it is conceded, as public responses to famine appeals would seem to suggest, that more could be done, a strong argument can be advanced for aid being provided as research expertise. Indeed, a policy statement of the AFRC, not so many years ago, stated 'Agricultural research is a valuable and relatively inexpensive form of aid creating self-reliance in the Third World'.[16] The BBSRC Corporate Plan does in fact make reference to developing countries, but its involvement in such research currently appears minimal, with only a proposal to 'continue to explore avenues for technology transfer and scientific collaboration with (developing countries)'. Moreover, it is a revealing fact that, uniquely among UK government ministries, the Overseas Development Administration (ODA) has no mission statement for its R & D (research and development), at a time when both the ODA and the British Council have been reducing university link funding with less-developed countries.[17]

But technology transfer to less-developed countries is by no means a simple issue. As argued persuasively by Susan George, the dominant Western agricultural model is often propagated in the Third World with harmful consequences. What is required is detailed critical evaluation of the relevance of Western science to the social, political and geographical environments of the specific countries concerned, that is, for a programme of 'research on research'.[18]

Acts of commission

Pursuing the approach to ethical analysis outlined in the ethical matrix (see chapter 7), it is apparent that several issues with an ethical dimension are included in BBSRC and MAFF policy statements. For example, one area of identified priority in the ASD statement is 'the physiological basis of stress in farm animals'. The terminology may differ, but without doubt BBSRC motives for wishing to enhance the welfare of animals kept in agricultural systems include respect for the principle of animal well-being.

But the inclusion of relevant research topics on policy programmes does not itself guarantee that ethical criteria are satisfied. So it is pertinent to ask three types of question if our ethical auditing is to be rigorous. First, is the topic assigned a priority, in terms of allocation of resources, commensurate with its ethical significance? Second, is the research addressing appropriate questions? Third, is the research conducted in a way which respects consumers' rights to know about the processes and products employed in food production?

With respect to the first question, the government body charged with responsibility for monitoring farm animal welfare and proposing research priorities is the Farm Animal Welfare Council (FAWC), an independent committee which periodically issues reports of its opinions on required research.[19] Both MAFF and the BBSRC acknowledge the importance of this source of advice. However, MAFF has allocated only 3% of its £127 million per annum research budget to animal welfare (compared with 47% on improving economic performance), and although animal welfare does feature in one of the eight initial areas in which the BBSRC is 'aligning our basic and strategic programmes with the needs of the user communities', it is included only in the programme for novel technologies for crop and livestock improvement, which might be considered an inappropriate context in which to address animal welfare concerns.

The second question raises conceptually more difficult issues. While it is widely recognised that animal captivity does not necessarily affect animal welfare adversely, reduced welfare is commonly associated with production systems which seek to enhance output (of milk, meat or eggs) per animal. There is thus frequently a lack of concurrence between the criteria for improved welfare perceived by producers (that which promotes high productivity) and that experienced by the animals. That the ASD sees welfare in the former sense is implied by the following statement:

> The impetus for this programme comes from the need to alleviate the increasing pressures that livestock are under as a result of the continuing quest for more efficient production of a product that meets the consumer's needs.[20]

But that assessment is open to question both because it seems to imply that the 'customer's needs' must necessarily take precedence over the animals' needs and because there is a growing appreciation among economists that animal welfare is an 'externality' which many consumers value. Thus, according to Colman: 'it might be said that competitive forces in agriculture have resulted in production systems in which the external costs [such as reduced animal welfare] are judged to be excessive by a significant number of the public. The growth of ethical demand by this group has outstripped the growth of ethical supply . . . '.[21]

The third question, concerning consumers' right to know about processes used in food production, falls within the remit of the Veterinary Medicines Directorate, a MAFF agency. The question prompts others, for example: when decisions are made about new products and practices affecting farm animal welfare, is the information supplied by scientists who are disinterested parties? The current requirement is for a manufacturer, say of a veterinary medical product, to submit an application for marketing authorisation to the government's Veterinary Products Committee (VPC), by whom it is assessed in terms of three criteria, namely, its quality, safety and efficacy. The relevant data are provided by the manufacturers, either from research carried out in-house or commissioned, for example in research institute laboratories. However, under Section 118 of the Medicines Act, signed by members of the VPC, it is illegal to declare publicly the reasons for approval or rejection of products. Respect for consumers' rights to know about products used in food production are therefore infringed.

Ethical concerns affecting consumer autonomy also arise from the increased commercialisation of research, as noted above.[22] As funds for public science decline, many scientists feel obliged to accept commercial funding to protect their livelihoods. But the effects on the practice of science of the transition from public to private sponsorship can be ethically significant. Results are no longer readily shared; and consequently they may be less open to the sceptical criticism which is an essential ingredient of theory testing. Moreover, commercially funded scientists clearly have a vested interest in the success of the product, and whether or not they are guilty of biased reporting, their statements are subject to widespread public distrust.[23]

Thus, consumers' rights to be informed about the processes involved in food production, which are jeopardised both by secrecy in regulation and by commercialisation, need to be respected by devising systems of testing which are patently open and fair. Some years ago, I suggested that this could be done by introducing a system of 'blind trials' in animal experimentation, placing the safety evaluation of veterinary products on a par with that of human medicines.[24]

SUSTAINABILITY

If there is one objective which more than most encompasses the ethical concerns inherent in modern agriculture it is 'sustainability'. While there is some philosophical debate about the precise definition of the term, essential features would seem to be those of reducing inputs (such as fossil fuels, pesticides, and artificial fertilisers) and conserving biodiversity and soil fertility.

The highly complex nature of the interaction between these objectives implies the need for holistic approaches to dealing with threats to sustainability, and the approach which commends itself to many is described by the term *organic farming*. Like sustainability, organic farming has numerous nuances (described, for example, as 'eco-farming' and 'permaculture'), but all share a common aim of avoiding reliance on chemical inputs and promoting extensive and humane systems of food production. MAFF's recent Research Strategy acknowledges that 'EU action on organic animal standards and planting materials could point to the need for more research and development in these areas'. But at a mere £1 million per annum,

MAFF's current support for research into organic systems hardly suggests that it is assigned a high priority.[25]

But traditional organic approaches to farming and food do not necessarily provide the soundest strategies for achieving sustainability. A generic term for the required type of holistic approach is 'systems approaches'. These involve the interaction of specialists (such as biologists, economists, sociologists and ethicists) in formulating appropriate questions, proposing, conducting and appraising relevant research and integrating the results. There is no intrinsic reason why such systems approaches should not combine biotechnology, information technology and robotic technology if they were employed in ways sensitive to the objectives of sustainability. Moreover, as Tom Blundell, Director General of the BBSRC, has pointed out, in relation to sustainable agriculture 'as in human medicine it is likely that many of the practically useful products of biotechnology will be in the areas of analysis and diagnostics rather than cure'.[26]

It is to be hoped that as the BBSRC develops its new strategies, a systems approach to sustainability will evolve. There are certainly encouraging signs in the statement that the ASD is to be 'distinctive in promoting a systems based approach, in which scientific innovation is tested in the context of the whole agricultural or biological system' and that it is to adopt a long-term view, looking to meet users' needs in five to twenty years' time.

EPISTEMOLOGY AND ETHICS

Up to this point in the discussion, there has been a tacit acceptance of the conventional wisdom on the nature of the relationship between science and technology, which has been described as the 'linear model'. According to this view, scientific research proceeds according to its own internal logic, producing neutral facts and explanatory schemata about the natural world, while technology consists of picking off the fruits which happenchance appear on this tree of knowledge. It is a view of the nature of science, characterised by Nicholas Maxwell as 'standard empiricism' (or the 'philosophy of knowledge').[27] Standard empiricism insists that the proper way to help promote human welfare is first to pursue the intellectual aim of acquiring knowledge, and only then to apply it to social problems. In attempting to procure scientific truth, all desires, fears, values, aspirations and problems of living are rigorously excluded from consideration. In other words, the needs of humanity are ignored so that the needs of humanity can be served!

Maxwell proposes an alternative approach ('aim-oriented rationalism' or 'the philosophy of wisdom') to achieving what is of value to us in life, the creation of a better world. In his view, absolute intellectual priority needs to be given to the tasks of: (i) articulating the problems we face; (ii) proposing and critically assessing possible solutions (personal and social actions); (iii) breaking up the problems into subordinate, specialised problems, such as those concerned with knowledge or technology; and (iv) synthesising the latter attempts in order to solve the major problems addressed. He admits that this would involve a revolution in the aims and methods of science, because rather than improving specialised knowledge the basic aim of intellectual enquiry would be that of enhancing social and personal wisdom, that is, helping to achieve what is of value in life for oneself and others.

According to Maxwell, the reason why standard empiricism (the view of science first propounded by Francis Bacon in the seventeenth century) prevails is that it has been allowed to commandeer every aspect of modern science, technology, scholarship and education. It determines what counts as academic enquiry, what constitutes valid criticism, what students are taught and who is appointed to prestigious academic positions.

It is impossible in the space available to do justice to Maxwell's arguments. But the suspicion that he may have a point is borne out by the insights of many others who have thought deeply about the practice of research. For example, consider Newby's comments on the effect of the linear model, which is, he claims, 'extremely difficult to dislodge in the minds of many senior agricultural policy makers':

> Once you get the science right, so the argument goes, better policy decisions are sure to follow. The task, not surprisingly, is seen as one for the scientific community. Expert panels of scientific peer review ensure that the science underlying agricultural policy is indeed 'right'. If the farming community fails to pick up the good science and translate it into leading edge farming practice, then that is the farming community's fault. ... The wider public is, of course, excluded from this process altogether. Its role is reduced to that of the hapless bystander or, later, the recipient of scientific advance which the scientific community believes it ought to want.[28]

The essential problem which Newby identifies is the emphasis in modern biology on reductionism. The newfound ability of scientists to manipulate genetic material and thus produce 'designer' organisms is just the latest step of a process in which biotic communities, societies and individuals are perceived merely as assemblages of molecules, susceptible to mechanistic laws.

An ethical approach to research policy may thus entail reappraisal of the aims and methods of enquiry to include a wider range of relevant issues. Agriculture and food production are, after all, human activities which impact on cultural, economic and social issues as well as biology: so why should we expect relevant research to be conducted almost exclusively by biologists? If, as Maxwell advocates, one started at the other end, seeking to enhance the ability to secure what is of human value, the research agenda might well be substantially different. Indeed, agricultural science can be conceived of as 'a social science, operating through the methods of natural science'.[29]

Research policy-makers might do well to consider the views of Paul Thompson, Director of the Centre for Biotechnology Policy and Ethics, and his colleague Bill Stout, at Texas A&M University:

> What's wrong with the agricultural research community? It's too damn scientific. It's not broad enough to consider social and ethical issues. Scientists are too far removed from the end use: they are ignorant of their own social context. Specialized language and concepts inhibit interdisciplinary research, to say nothing of the dialogue with non-specialists. Specialization is the only way we know how to do science, but agricultural science should include humanistic specialists as well.[30]

CONCLUSIONS

Research into food production and processing has proved to be the engine of change in the food industry. It has had profound effects on the quantity and quality of food available, on the number and nature of jobs available, on the lives of animals reared for food, on the ecology and appearance of the rural environment and on the very way in which people consume their food. Yet many of the changes introduced would not have been chosen had society been fully aware of the implications of the scientific research on which they were based. Discussion in this chapter has been limited to very few examples, for example, those concerning animal welfare, but ethical concerns are evident throughout the food industry.

In the brave new world of GATT, with its relentless emphasis on global competitiveness, there seems to be an even greater potential than hitherto for infringing ethical principles relating to food production and availability on a global scale. But since it would be grossly irresponsible to simply 'give up' in the face of such seemingly intractable problems, particularly by those who have benefitted from agricultural research while others have suffered, there is an ethical imperative to address these issues with urgency. Of all the strategies for addressing problems such as these, greater investment in appropriate research would seem to promise the soundest hope of success. And if that is so, there can be no greater priority than that of formulating research policies which as far as possible have been ethically audited.

NOTES

1 Newby, H. (1993) 'The social shaping of agriculture: where do we go from here?' *Journal of the Royal Agricultural Society of England* 154, 9–18.

2 Thompson, P.B., *The Spirit of the Soil: agriculture and environmental ethics* (London, Routledge, 1995).

3 Ibid.

4 Webster, A., *Science, Technology and Society* (Basingstoke, Macmillan, 1991) p.34.

5 'Realising our potential: a strategy for science, engineering and technology', Cm 2250, London, HMSO, 1993.

6 Blundell, T. (Chief Executive of the BBSRC), Foreword to *BBSRC Corporate Plan (1995–1999)* (Swindon, Biotechnology and Biological Sciences Research Council) p.2.

7 In 1995, the Office of Science and Technology published reports, entitled *Progress Through Partnership*, of the Technology Foresight panels on 'Food and Drink' (vol. 7), and on 'Agriculture, Natural Resources and the Environment' (vol. 11) (London, HMSO, 1995).

8 As described in the *BBSRC Corporate Plan 1995–1999* (Swindon, Biotechnology and Biological Sciences Research Council); and in *MAFF Research Strategy* (London, Ministry of Agriculture, Fisheries and Food, 1995). All subsequent references to the BBSRC and MAFF refer to these publications unless otherwise stated.

9 For example, the MAFF committees on the *Ethics of Genetic Modification of Food* (1993) and *Ethical Implications of Emerging Technologies in the Breeding of Farm Animals* (1995); and the Nuffield Council on Bioethics committees on *Genetic Screening* (1993), *Human Tissue* (1995), and *Xenotransplantation* (1996).

10   Snow, C.P., *The Two Cultures and the Scientific Revolution: The Rede Lecture 1959* (Cambridge, Cambridge University Press, 1959).

11   Accessible sources of information on global, population and resource trends are: Harrison, P., *The Third Revolution* (Harmondsworth, Penguin, 1992); and Kennedy, P., *Preparing for the Twenty-First Century* (London, Fontana, 1994).

12   Drèze, J. and Sen, A., *Hunger and Public Action* (Oxford, Clarendon Press, 1989) p.3.

13   Alston, P., quoted in Chen, R.S. and Kates, R.W. (1994) 'World food security: prospects and trends', *Food Policy* 19, 192–208.

14   'Realising our Potential . . .', op. cit., pp.29–31.

15   Department of Education and Employment (1995) *Press Notice 5.7.95* (London, 10 Downing Street).

16   Agricultural and Food Research Council, *A long-term view of the agricultural and food research service* (London, AFRC, 1985) p.3.

17   The SET Forum, *Shaping the Future* (Milton Keynes, Open University, 1995).

18   George, S., *Ill Fares the Land* (London, Writers and Readers, 1989) p.60.

19   Farm Animal Welfare Council, *Priorities in Animal Welfare R & D* (Surbiton, FAWC, 1993).

20   Agricultural Systems Directorate (ASD) *Strategy* (1995), Annex 1A, p.2.

21   Colman, D. (1994) 'Ethics and externalities: agricultural stewardship and other behaviour – presidential address', *Journal of Agricultural Economics* 45, 299–331.

22   Webster, A., op. cit.

23   For example, only 1% of people canvassed in the EU cited 'industry' as the most reliable source of information on biotechnology (compared with 27% who cited consumer associations); see Marlier, E., 'Eurobarometer 35.1', in *Biotechnology in Public*, Durant, J. (ed.) (London, Science Museum, 1992).

24   Mepham, T.B., 'Criteria for the public acceptability of biotechnological innovations in animal production', in *Biotechnology in Growth Regulation*, Heap, R.B., Prosser, C.G. and Lamming, G.E. (eds) (London, Butterworths, 1989) pp.203–212.

25   MAFF, *MAFF-sponsored Research into Organic Farming* (London, MAFF, 1994) p.1.

26   Blundell, T. (1993) 'New scientific opportunities for sustainable agriculture', *Journal of the Royal Agricultural Society of England* 154, 19–28.

27   Maxwell, N., *From Knowledge to Wisdom* (Oxford, Blackwell, 1984).

28   Newby, H., op. cit.

29   Krohn, W. and Schafer, W., 'Agricultural chemistry: a goal oriented science', in *Science in Context*, Barnes, B. and Edge, D. (eds) (Milton Keynes, Open University Press, 1982) pp.196–211.

30   Stout, B.A. and Thompson, P.B., in *Beyond the Large Farm*, Thompson, P.B. and Stout, B.A. (eds) (Boulder, CO, Westview Press, 1991) p.276.

Select bibliography
Fifty key references

Aiken, W. and La Follette, H. (eds) *World Hunger and Moral Obligation*, 2nd edn (Englewood Cliffs, Prentice Hall, 1995).

Beck, U., *The Risk Society* (London, Sage, 1992).

Beck, U., *Organized Irresponsibility* (London, Polity Press, 1994).

Beitz, C., *Political Theory and International Relations*, Part III (Princeton, Princeton University Press, 1979).

Blatz, C.V. (ed.) *Ethics and Agriculture: an anthology on world issues in current context* (Moscow, Idaho, University of Idaho Press, 1991).

Busch, L., Lacy, W.B., Burkhardt, J. and Lacy, L.R., *Plants, Power and Profit: social, economic and ethical consequences of the new biotechnologies* (Cambridge MA, Blackwell, 1992).

Cannon, D., *The Politics of Food* (London, Century, 1986).

Craig Smith, N. and Quelch, J.A., *Ethics in Marketing* (Boston MA, Irwin, 1993).

Crawford, M.A. and Marsh, D.E.,*Nutrition and Evolution* (New Canaan, Keats Publishing, 1995).

Curtin, D.W. and Heldke, L.M., *Cooking, Eating, Thinking: transformative philosophies of food* (Bloomington and Indianapolis, Indiana University Press, 1992).

Dower, N., *World Poverty: challenge and response* (York, Sessions, 1983).

Douglas, M., *Risk and Blame* (London, Routledge, 1992).

Drèze, J. and Sen, A., *The Political Economy of Hunger* (Cambridge, Cambridge University Press, 1990).

Durning, A.B. and Brough, H.B., *Taking Stock: animal farming and the environment*, Worldwatch Paper 103, (Washington DC, Worldwatch Institute, 1991).

Eason, R.J., Pada, J., Wallace, R., Henry, A. and Thornton, R. (1987) 'Changing patterns of hypertension, diabetes, obesity and diet among Melanesians and Micronesians in the Solomon Islands', *Medical Journal of Australia* 146, 465–473.

Elias, N., *The Civilizing Process: Volume 1, The History of Manners* (London, Blackwell, 1978).

Evans, L.T., *Crop Evolution, Adaptation and Yield* (Cambridge, Cambridge University Press, 1993).

Food and Agriculture Organisation/World Health Organisation, *Conjoint Expert Consultation: The Role of Dietary Fats and Oils in Human Nutrition* (Rome, FAO, 1995).

Fiddes, N., *Meat: a natural symbol* (London, Routledge 1991).

Gendel, S.M., Kline, A.D., Warren, D.M. and Yates, F. (eds) *Agricultural Bioethics: implications of agricultural biotechnology* (Ames, Iowa State University Press, 1990).

Garrot, G.R., *Ethics in Business: a deeper approach. Your Guide to the New Era in Business* (Hobart, Tasmania, Institute of Business Ethics Inc., 1992).

Goodman, D. and Redclift, M., *Refashioning Nature: food, ecology and culture* (London, Routledge, 1991).

Guyomard, H., Mahle, L., Munk, K. and Roe, T.L. (1993) 'Agriculture in the Uruguay Round: ambitions and realities', *Journal of Agricultural Economics* 44, 245–263.

Harriss-White, B. and Hoffenberg, R. (eds) *Food: multidisciplinary perspectives* (Oxford UK and Cambridge USA, Blackwell, 1993).

Jackson, W., *New Roots for Agriculture* (Lincoln and London, University of Nebraska Press, 1985).

Johnson, A., *Factory Farming* (Oxford, Blackwell, 1991).

Kloppenberg, J.R. Jr, *First the Seed: the political economy of plant biotechnology* (Cambridge, Cambridge University Press, 1988) pp.1492–2000.

Krimsky, S. and Wrubel, R. *Agricultural Biotechnology and the Environment: science, policy and social issues* (Urbana and Chicago, Univeristy of Illinois Press, 1996).

LeMay, B.W.J. (ed.) *Science, Ethics and Food* (Washington DC, Smithsonian Institution Press, 1988).

Mennell, S., Murcott, A. and Van Otterloo, A.H., *The Sociology of Food, Eating, Diet and Culture* (London, Sage/International Sociological Association, 1992).

Mepham, T.B., Tucker, G.A. and Wiseman, J. (eds) *Issues in Agricultural Bioethics* (Nottingham, Nottingham University Press, 1995).

Millstone, E., 'Consumer protection policies in the EC: the quality of food', in Freeman, C. *et al.* (eds) *Technology and the Future of Europe* (London, Pinter, 1991) ch. 20.

Millstone, E., 'Can the political role of science be democratised, and if so how?', in Goncalves, M.E. (ed.) *Ciencia and Democracia* (Lisbon, Portuguese Federation of Scientific Societies, 1996).

Ministry of Agriculture, Fisheries and Food, *Report of the Committee to Consider the Ethical Implications of Emerging Technologies in the Breeding of Farm Animals* (London, HMSO, 1995).

National Research Council, *Alternative Agriculture* (Washington DC, National Academy Press, 1989).

Persley, G.J., *Beyond Mendel's Garden: biotechnology in the service of world agriculture* (Wallingford, CAB International for the World Bank, 1990).

Pimentel, D. and Lehman, H. (eds) *The Pesticide Question: environment, economics and ethics* (New York, Chapman and Hall, 1993).

Regan, T., *The Case for Animal Rights* (London, Routledge, 1983).

Schwartz, M. and Thompson, M., *Divided We Stand: redefining politics, technology and social choice* (London, Harvester Wheatsheaf, 1990).

Serpell, J., *In the Company of Animals* (Oxford, Blackwell, 1986).

Shue, H., *Basic Rights: subsistence, affluence and US foreign policy* (Princeton, Princeton University Press, 1980).

Soloman, R.C., *Ethics and Excellence: cooperation and integrity in business* (New York, Oxford University Press, 1992).

Soule, J.D. and Piper, J.K., *Farming in Nature's Image: an ecological approach to agriculture* (Washington DC, Island Press, 1992).

Thomas, K., *Man and the Natural World* (London, Allen Lane, 1985).

Thompson, P.B., *The Ethics of Aid and Trade: US food policy, foreign competition and the social contract* (New York, Cambridge University Press, 1992).

Thompson, P.B., *The Spirit of the Soil: agriculture and environmental ethics* (London, Routledge, 1995).

Thompson, P.B. and Stout, B.A. (eds) *Beyond the Large Farm: ethics and research goals for agriculture* (Boulder, Colorado, Westview Press, 1991).

Thompson, P.B., Matthews, R.J. and van Ravenswaay, E.O., *Ethics, Public Policy and Agriculture* (New York, Macmillan, 1994).

Tracy, M., *Agriculture in Western Europe: challenge and response 1880–1980*, 2nd edn (London, Granada, 1982).

Ucko, P.J. and Dimbleby, G.W., *The Domestication and Exploitation of Plants and Animals* (London, Duckworth, 1969).

Index

additives 72, 138, 140, 141, 149, 150–1; acceptable daily intake 144–5; health risk from 72, 96–8, 142–6
Advertising Standards Authority (UK) 141–2
Advisory Committee on Novel Foods and Processes (ACNFP) (UK) 101, 113
Africa 27, 69, 37, 65, 66, 67, 76, 77, 78, 159
Agricultural and Food Research Council (AFRC) (UK) 156–7, 161
agricultural labourforce 20, 26, 156
agricultural policy 155–6, 166
Agricultural Systems Directorate (UK) *see* Biotechnology and Biological Sciences Research Council
Agriculture Act 1947 (UK) 155
aid policy 5
Alar 150
animal: experiments 66, 93–6, 110, 142–3, 144, 164; rights 51, 130–1, 133; selective breeding 57, 70, 102, 129; trade in 27, 58, 134; transgenesis 114–16; welfare 50, 54, 55–8, 60–2, 86, 106, 108–9, 112, 115, 129–31, 134–5, 146–7, 148, 150–1, 156, 159, 162–3, 168
anorexia 124
Aristotelian ethics 12–13
Asia 37, 76, 77, 78
Asp, E. 125

Atwater, W.O. 66
Australia 44, 65
autonomy, principle of 105–6

Bacon, Francis 166
Beauchamp, T.L. 104–5
Beardsworth, A. 128
Beck, U. 121
Beitz, C. 14
Beltsville pigs 114
beneficence, principle of 105–6
Benhabib, S. 135
Bentham, Jeremy 52
biodiversity 21, 40, 59, 106, 111, 164
biomass 38, 55
bioreactors 114
biota 111
biotechnology 101–17, 121, 132–4, 158, 159, 165, 167; regulation 102, 103, 116–17
Biotechnology and Biological Sciences Research Council (BBSRC) 156–7, 161–3, 165
biotic community 106
Blanchard, K. 139, 142, 147
Blundell, T. 165
bovine somatotrophin (BST) 58, 107–12, 114, 115–16, 120, 151
bovine spongiform encephalopathy (BSE) 70–1; 91–2, 120
Brazil 77
breastmilk 75, 151
British Columbia 123
British Council 162

North American Free Trade Area
(NAFTA) 28
Norway 75
Nussbaum, M.C. 12
nutrition 13, 64–79, 127, 129, 141;
see also malnutrition

obligation, theories of 10–15
Office of Fair Trading (UK) 141
Office of Science and Technology
(UK) 161
O'Neill, O. 10
organic: farming 43, 61, 97, 150, 157,
164–5; food 61, 86, 111, 140, 141,
147–8
Organisation for Economic Co-
operation and Development
(OECD) 23
organo-phosphates 91; *see also*
pesticides
osteoporosis 110
Overseas Development
Administration (ODA) 161–2

Pahl, R. 126
Peale 139, 142, 147
pesticides 20, 43, 55, 91, 146, 149–51,
164
Phillipines 45
Phytophthora infestans 41; *see also*
famine, Irish Potato Famine
pigs 55, 57, 59, 69, 122, 146
plant breeding 40–1, 42, 102
Plutarch 61
Pogge, T. 14
Polkinghorne Committee 101, 114,
132
pollution 20–1, 44, 59, 79, 111, 146,
156
polychlorinated biphenyls (PCBs)
72
polyphosphates 72
Posilac 108; *see also* bovine
somatotrophin
poultry 56, 59, 129; *see also* chickens
poverty 1–16, 24, 65, 77; and hunger
1, 2, 7–9
prima facie duties 105–7, 159

Ravetz, J.R. 139
Rawls, John 14–15, 30, 50, 106; *see
also* contractualism
Regan, T. 51
regionality 44
research policy 158–64
rights 30, 50–1; *see also* animal
rights, deontology and human
rights
Ritzer, G. 131–2
Roberts, P. 62
Robertson Smith, W. 121
Roethlisberger, F.J. 139
Rothamsted Experimental Station
(UK) 35, 36, 44
Rousseau, Jean-Jacques 50
Royal College of Physicians (UK) 70

saccharin 89–98, 144
Safeway stores 150
Sale of Food and Drugs Act 1875
(UK) 85
Salsburg, D. 94
Samuel, R. 131
Saudi Arabia 76
Schwartz, M. 88
science and technology policy 156
Scotland 68
Sen, A. 12, 121
Sennauer, A. 125
Sharratt 94
Shue, H. 13, 15
Singer, P. 11–12, 52, 138
Slaughter House Act 1974 (UK) 58
Snow, C.P. 158
social ethics 104
soil 36–9, 46, 59, 79, 111, 164
Soil Conservation Service (USA) 38
soil degradation 21, 36–9, 43, 58, 59,
65, 146, 160
Solomon Islands 69
Spain 58
Spongiform Encephalopathy
Advisory Committee (UK) 71
Stout, B.A. 167
South Africa 27, 69
South America 65, 76, 77
subsistence agriculture 41, 76
sugar 73, 76–7